THE BATTLE OF BROOKLYN,
1776

THE
BATTLE OF
Brooklyn
1776

John J. Gallagher

CASTLE BOOKS

This edition published in 2002 by Castle Books ®
A division of Book Sales, Inc.
114 Northfield Avenue, Edison, NJ 08837

This edition published by arrangement with and permission of
De Capo Press, a subsidiary of
Perseus Books L.L.C.
387 Park Avenue South
New York, New York 10016-8810

Library of Congress Cataloging-in-Publication Data
Gallagher, John J., 1937-
    The Battle of Brooklyn 1776/ John J. Gallagher
        p.   cm.
    Includes bibliographical references and index.
    1. Long Island (N.Y.), Battle of, 1776. I. Title.
    E241.L8G35 1995
    973.3'32—dc20   95-712
                                                            CIP

ISBN: 0-7858-1663-1

Printed in the United States of America

This book is dedicated to
Herb Yellin,
gentleman, scholar and
foremost historian of the Battle of Brooklyn.

Contents

Preface

A T ONE TIME I might have concurred with the considerable number of people who have underestimated the Battle of Brooklyn as
a seminal event in both American and Western history. In fact, more
accurately, I was one of the even greater number who did not give "The
Battle of Long Island," as it has been called, much thought at all.

Because a Brooklyn historian requested that I lend a military history
perspective to a lecture event that was to commemorate the battle,
however, I found myself compelled to delve into the events of August
27, 1776. It quickly became apparent to me that the clash of main British
and colonial forces in North America that day comprised not only a
major event in the War of Independence, but marked an important
transition in the history of warfare as well. With this battle, the days of
the chivalric contest-cum-display staged by the monarchs of Europe had
ended. With democratic principles having come into play, the nature
of military conflict had shifted in an entirely new direction.

This is not to say that the fighting in Brooklyn *caused* an historic
change in the behavior of nations—though important lessons were
learned that day. More to the point, the great clash in Brooklyn
inaugurated a new age of warfare. The battle marked the first step,
however tenuous, into the modern era of "total" war.

The military engagement that many historians call the Battle of
Long Island was, naturally, fought there. Brooklyn as a borough was not
yet in existence. But the battle should have had a more local name—
indeed, earlier writers did call it "The Battle of/at/for Brooklyn." Just

as the Battle of Bunker Hill did not rage throughout Massachusetts, the battle staged in Brooklyn did not extend throughout Long Island. Although the area covered by the fighting was extensive for those times—at least twice that covered by the Battle of Waterloo, for example—the fighting took place over not much more than half the area of today's Brooklyn. It all occurred in the space of one morning, and the concentration of combat—and casualties—would be surpassed by no other battle of the war.

The practice in Europe was to name a battle after the nearest major settlement. Waterloo was fought about one and a half miles south of Waterloo village, at La Haye Sainte. This was more or less the same distance from the settled part of the Town of Brooklyn where the major fighting took place: Flatbush Pass and the Old Stone House at Gowanus. Howe's dispatch on the British victory was marked "Long Island"—a generality; Wellington's was written at Waterloo.

In 1776, the eastern boundary of the Town of Brooklyn lay at the foot of the Flatbush Pass, marked by the Dongan Oak, which the Americans cut down during the fight to form a barrier across the Flatbush Road; the southern boundary was at today's 60th Street, almost a mile south of the watermelon patch where the first shots of the battle were fired. To the east, the township boundary encompassed the village of Bedford.

The historian Henry Stiles wrote in 1867: "We have preferred to call this the 'Battle of Brooklyn,' because that term more completely describes the *locale* of the battle which was fought entirely within the limits of the old town, now included in the present day city of Brooklyn." And Martha Bockée Flint wrote in 1895: "Now began the stirring events of the week whose culminating action is recorded in history as the Battle of Long Island, a misnomer for what contemporary writing and tradition always call the Battle of Brooklyn." In 1951, the United States government legitimized the title when it issued a three-cent stamp, "The Battle of Brooklyn," which depicted Washington mounted on a white horse, directing the action from atop a ridge.

Of what actually happened on August 27, 1776, I have tried to write as objective an account as I can. Original sources have been drawn upon whenever possible and I have done my best to be conscientious in citing references. I trust historians will not be too harsh with me should they find any lapse, and I also trust this book will prompt others to search for more information to fill in any blank spaces that still exist in the history of the battle.

The opinions stated in the book are my own or are identified as those of others whose names I mention. I have walked over the battlefield and the places mentioned, from the Rockaways to Willett's Point, to see whether the movements were possible in the times mentioned by other authors. I have noted the appearance of the sites, measured the distances and elevations and taken into account previous observations, to describe what I see as the geographic actualities of the battle.

There are other accounts of the battle that cite numbers, dates, troop movements and heroic acts with an admirable attention to detail. I have also tried to tell the larger story. What follows is a case history designed to illustrate the theory that the face of warfare changed suddenly during those few hours on a summer day over 200 years ago. The first battle fought by the first modern democracy may have resulted in a defeat for its citizen-soldiers, but their valiant effort signaled the beginning of the end of an old European order and the start of the age of the Rights of Man.

Foreword

O N A WALK THROUGH Brooklyn on a hot August day, anybody's imagination would be stretched trying to visualize another summer day over two hundred years ago, when tens of thousands of soldiers fought to decide the fate of America. On August 27, 1776, a crucial battle of the Revolutionary War was fought on Brooklyn's soil, nearly resulting in the decisive defeat of George Washington's Continental Army. Both the professional soldiers of the Old World and the citizen soldiers of the New marched, fought and died through the present-day neighborhoods of Bedford-Stuyvesant, Crown Heights, Fort Greene, Flatbush, Park Slope, Cobble Hill and others, as well as in what are now Prospect Park and Green-Wood Cemetery.

Historians have long been interested not only in remembering battles, but in noting how and why they have been commemorated. The wars and battles a culture retains and embroiders in its popular imagination are no more revealing than those that are neglected or forgotten. In sharp contrast to the hundreds of monuments and elaborate interpretive displays at, for example, Gettysburg and Valley Forge, the battlefield of Brooklyn is marked only by a few modest physical reminders. Battles and battlefields become part of our national heritage because people wish to pay tribute to martial courage and perpetuate a sense of connection to the living past. The Battle of Brooklyn, however, seems to have disappeared long ago from our nation's consciousness.

In line with current patriotic canon, for homage to a battlefield to occur it is vital that the physical space of the site be sharply defined and the ground be considered, to some degree, sacred. In Brooklyn, it is true, the few remaining traces of sacred space have been rendered nearly invisible. The Maryland Brigade fought a heroic, but hopeless rearguard action on the day of the battle. Its counterattacks occurred in the area of the present-day Old Stone House, located in J.J. Byrne Park in Park Slope near the Gowanus Canal. The present building is not the exact house used in the battle, but it is a close enough reconstruction. That it is soon to be turned into a historical resource center has only occurred because a few determined individuals have fought to make that happen. They are working to increase and share knowledge, not only of the battle, but of the American Revolution and our common heritage. For its part, the Old Stone House has been used over the generations as, variously, a public bathroom, a meeting hall, a shop and a storage facility.

If the dead at the Alamo were discovered to be buried under an auto repair shop, such a desecration would not long be allowed to stand. But many of the Maryland dead lie today under the roof of such an establishment, the deed of which property once stipulated that their burial place be undisturbed. Even as the battle itself has dimmed in our memory, so has the sacrifice of some of the bravest of our patriots.

While Americans today may view the Revolution as a distant, and even anachronistic, event, the fewer than three million who lived through it endured a grim and difficult trial. To place its contemporary impact in perspective, one needs only to look at the casualties. Approximately 25,000 Americans were killed in combat, and from captivity and disease. In modern terms, this represents the equivalent of two million dead. Roughly 150,000 to 200,000 Americans fought in the American Revolution. The percentage of those under arms increases when the militias assigned to home defenses are included. If we include the half a million Loyalists among the population, and a similar number of African-Americans — many of whom, in bondage, were participants nonetheless — the numbers are even higher. The Native American population primarily sided with the British; and a bitter war-within-a-war was waged between the rebelling colonists and "Loyalist" Indians. For those engulfed in the passions of the times, the Revolution increasingly became our first civil war. This was especially true when the British began focusing their attention on the American South after 1778.

During 1775–76, the American colonies suffered a string of defeats, including the unsuccessful invasion of Canada, the battles of Brooklyn, Manhattan and White Plains, and Washington's retreat into New Jersey. The grand army assembled by Washington to meet the British in Brooklyn almost disappeared. It declined from over 20,000 in September 1776 to less than 4,000 by December, when the dramatic battles of Trenton and Princeton were fought. (For the attack on Trenton, Washington had to plead with several units to stay a few days beyond their enlistment time.) These losses were by and large the result of discouragement—the impact of successive defeats with concurrent disillusionment and a growing rate of desertion—and the departure of soldiers, and indeed whole units, who returned home at the end of their short-term enlistments. The performance of many militia units at the Battle of Brooklyn prompted the Continental Congress to establish the standing army Washington had long argued for. Indeed, the disintegration over the next few months of the number of soldiers in the field *forced* the Congress to face the imperative of creating a regular army.

As shown by the Battle of Brooklyn, the Revolution, if successful, would be won as a war of the thirteen colonies united as a nation, with an army representing the whole, not parts of it, or factions, each with its own contribution to make but also with its own local agenda. In fact, from the earliest times of European settlement on this continent until today, the question of the role of citizen soldiers versus a professional army as the bulwark of our defense has bedeviled those who determine our approach to warfare. The New World, after all, has never been saddled with the military traditions of the Old. In the period of the Enlightenment—when American political thought truly began—a standing army was considered unacceptable; it would have been evidence of an immoral—or un-Loyal—body politic. In contrast, the self-sacrificing individual who exhibited his civic virtue by participating in a militia was seen as expressing the highest form of citizenship. With the Battle of Brooklyn, the Congress was forced to reassess its thoughts about a national, standing army.

In practice, the militia performed best as a defensive force, useful for maintaining social control and regulating slaves, but also potentially fractious if political winds blew the wrong way—and in the early days of the Revolution, these winds swept a number of militia units and collections of local Loyalists into coalition with the British. Aside from its lack of military effectiveness, Washington and other political-military leaders did not want to rely on a militia-based army because it might threaten to turn the Revolution into an uncontrolled civil conflict characterized by guerrilla-style warfare.

As John Gallagher demonstrates in this book, the first large battle fought by the American nation was nearly its last. Long a student of military history, and the Battle of Brooklyn in particular, he has given us a work that will spur further investigation of this dramatic encounter that came perilously close to a total disaster for the new army of the thirteen colonies. After a reading of this book, the sites and topography of Brooklyn will doubtless take on new meaning for those unaware of the heritage of that city. No longer, it is hoped, will reference to the Battle of Brooklyn be met with blank stares or the vague assumption that it labels some gang fight, urban unpleasantness or Dodger game.

The largest battle of the Revolutionary War makes for a dramatic story that comprises part of the spiritual heritage of all Americans. New Yorkers, nevertheless, may feel a particular pride in learning—if they already have not—that the borough called Brooklyn has undeniable claim to be honored as hallowed ground.

James Dingeman
New York, January 1995

INTRODUCTION

"Democratic Warfare"

THE STATUE OF LIBERTY in New York harbor faces a hill in Brooklyn. It was a gift from the people of France to honor, in words spoken at its dedication, the first blow for human liberty and democracy in modern times. Directly across the bay, facing the French statue — "Liberty Enlightening the World," to use its full title — is the Altar to Liberty, erected by Charles M. Higgins, of India Ink fame and wealth, in 1920.

The Brooklyn hill is in the Green-Wood Cemetery, close to where, around 10 P.M. on August 26, 1776, an American rifleman exchanged fire with a party of British foragers gathering watermelon, a delicacy they had never seen in England. It was the month after the united colonies had declared their independence, and the age of the great "democratic wars" had begun with one pull of the trigger.

The Battle of Brooklyn was the first general engagement between large, organized armies in the first of all the great "participatory" patriotic wars to come. It was the first time the fledgling Continental Army acted as the agent of an independent nation, one founded on democratic principles. The battle was fought by men with a cause they were willing to die for. They faced an army of professional soldiers more used to fighting other professionals in the familial, territorial and commercial disputes of their employers — the so-called "cabinet wars" that followed the brutal ravages of the Thirty Years' War (1618–48). The Americans of the New World were in the process of developing new values; the British were defending traditional ones.

1

The action on August 27, 1776, was the largest battle of the American Revolution in terms of both participants and casualties. In Brooklyn, both sides had hopes of ending the conflict with one great victory, and massed their forces accordingly. As it turned out, however, the British were able to bring to bear nearly all their 32,000 men while the Americans employed 11,000, only part of their strength and just a fraction of their force as it looked on paper. (At Yorktown, by comparison, both sides totaled only 19,000.)

The battle was fought in the old, almost ritualistic European style, albeit with some unique twists peculiar to the military novices of the thirteen colonies. Since the American rebellion, to British eyes, combined aspects of both a colonial war and an insurrection, the fact that rules of engagement nevertheless echoed more closely practices established on the battlefields of Europe was a fortunate development. Both British and American military experience in the New World, after all, had not always been so "civilized."

In Britain's intercolonial wars against France—that is, wars fought outside of Europe but on behalf of colonial interests—prisoners were an inconvenience (unless they were women, hostages or slaves—positions often interchangeable), and village burnings, depredations and massacres were commonplace. Because "savages" were the victims—be they white, red or black, and because hostilities were two to three months away as news traveled—sensibilities in Europe were not too much offended.* At the beginning of the American Revolution, memories of the atrocities of former wars haunted the British. After all, the great preponderance of what little military experience the Americans had had was in fighting

---

*Although what went on in the intercolonial wars was usually ignored in Europe, one incident attracted such close attention that it is credited to be the spark that ignited the Seven Years' War (1756–63). In General Edward Braddock's campaign against Fort Duquesne in 1755, a French diplomat empowered to negotiate a ceasefire was killed by an Indian fighting alongside the British. This happened when the Frenchman was being given safe conduct by George Washington, then an aide to Braddock, and with the Indian under Washington's command. However, just as the First World War was not actually *caused* by the assassination of an Austrian Archduke in Sarajevo, it would not be fair to lay at young Washington's feet the responsibility for a global conflict. The young officer's gaffe simply focused contentions that had been growing between the European powers.

Indians—usually a village burning to drive them farther west—and in such wars rules were relaxed, if applied at all.

But while the British might have worried over facing an opponent steeped in frontier-style barbarity, the other fact influencing the rules of engagement was the idea of insurrection. The rebels were striking at the Monarch and in turn, probably, the divine right of all monarchs. Had any of the signers of the Declaration of Independence fallen under the power of the British there was a very good chance they would have been shot, as were many of the participants in the next direct insurrection the British faced, that of the Irish during the Easter Rising in 1916.

Actions prior to the Battle of Brooklyn had done little to establish exactly what sort of war the British and Americans would be engaged in. One effect of the battle was to establish that—much to the relief of many participants—the Americans were not bent on playing by "frontier" rules, and on the other hand, the British were now fighting a country and not just a mob.

*   *   *

In the beginning, the American "question" was one of Englishmen seeking their rights and addressing their grievances to the Monarch because Parliament had turned a deaf ear to their earlier pleas.

Unlike the administrators and merchants who went out to rule and trade in a reasonably settled colony—dealing with existing civilizations of varying form, making their money and returning home—the American colonists generally went for good. They established families, farms, towns and cities. They were settlers in the truest sense of the word. They looked to the New World and had cut most of their ties to the Old. Apart from a connection often at most sentimental, they had signed their bargain with the new land.

The political arrangement was divided. The settlers, mostly from the British Isles, with a dense cluster of Germans and spots of other groups, were living under a colonial administration. Royal Governors were sent out from the Motherland as well as troops, whose costs the British Government was trying to have the colonists take a greater share in—but without representation or much influence in Parliament.

The commercial relationship was close, fostered by the mercantile system of the 17th and 18th centuries. However, even though it was dependent for luxuries and manufactured goods shipped on twice-annual fleets from Britain, America was becoming more and more self-sufficient, or at least trying to, with a growing small manufacturing industry and a thriving practice in smuggling (in an effort to contravene the Navigation Acts, which gave British shipping almost a monopoly on American trade). At the same time, English commercial patterns were shifting away from North America to new colonies and opportunities elsewhere.

The American colonists, in fact, had very few friends in London. The West Indies was the largest source of profit to England and commanded, through financial interests and commercial connections, close to 100 seats in Parliament, almost one-quarter of the vote at the time. Requests and legal remonstrances from the Americans had no effect on that deliberative body despite debates led by such men as Edmund Burke, Charles Fox, John Wilkes, Isaac Barre, and the Howe brothers— Admiral Lord Richard and General Sir William.

By the time of the Battle of Brooklyn, remonstrances were useless. The Declaration of Independence had been ratified by the united colonies and these had indeed become the United States, although that name had yet to be established.

In his *On War,* published in 1832, Karl von Clausewitz noted that the conduct of any war is dependent on three elements: the government, the army and the people. To Clausewitz, who based his observations on his experience during the Napoleonic wars, the government determines the objectives of the war— to win, to contain, or simply to resist; the army prosecutes the war; and the people support or endure it. Prior to the American Revolution, the third element was seldom a major factor, unless there were too few young men to fill the ranks, or the populace was so ravaged that it could no longer tolerate the conflict.

With the American Revolution, the support of the people became a major factor. In this respect, through genuine patriotic fervor, group allegiance or, in some number of cases, coercion, the people were for the most part in agreement, and mobilized— at least in spirit— for the struggle. Heretofore, a European army could march at will, living, if need be, off the land as it went, hindered only by an opposing force. With the advent of an army with great popular support, the sterile maneuvers of earlier armies—often a monarch's expensive personal property—became impracticable. The British found, in this fight against a people with a participatory democracy, such earlier freedom of movement to be impossible. During the Revolution they could only hold port cities, and that only because of the might of the Royal Navy, which provided supply and communications by sea and overwhelming artillery support when the target was in range of its ships.

The first shots fired in the American Revolution were at the battles of Lexington and Concord, some fifteen months before the Declaration of Independence, little more than guerrilla warfare by a handful of farmers shooting at British columns from behind rocks, walls and trees. The Americans had very good organization for this type of fighting and enjoyed excellent intelligence—accurate knowledge of British intentions and movements. Lexington and Concord proved that Americans could fight irregular warfare, evolving tactics that would greatly contribute to eventual victory. Bunker Hill subsequently proved that Americans could dig in and tenaciously defend field fortifications. Other early actions included surprise attacks, sieges, assaults on fortifications and tentative efforts at fighting in line, particularly in Canada, involving at most a few thousand men. Everything the Americans had done so far, politically and militarily, led up to the Battle of Brooklyn.

In this battle, a new type of warfare was born, that of a massive democratic army fighting for a belief, and both killing and being killed in ever-growing numbers. The American Revolution marked the beginning of the great patriotic wars, in which entire populations would be pitted against each other rather than just armies. The scope of the fighting would eventually grow to threaten not only civilians at home but, in its ultimate manifestation, nuclear weapons, even those who would be born well after the fighting ended.

The idea of citizens giving their all for patriotic reasons, first expressed in the American Revolution, was improved upon by the great levies of the French Revolution and the Napoleonic wars. It was refined during the U.S. Civil War to deliberately involve *all* of the enemy's civilian population. According to Northern General William Tecumseh Sherman, "war is not popularity seeking." He wrote that the enemy was a "hostile people,"[1] not just the army facing him; and he defined terror against civilians as a weapon. There had also been reprisals against civilians during the American Revolution, but these were more a reflection of both the irregular nature of fighting in the vast forests of the New World and British frustrations with sporadic actions by local commanders (much like later reprisals in Vietnam) than an official war policy. The escalation of patriotic warfare reached its military maturity in the First World War, and its apex of destruction with the air raids of the Second, with their aim, obliteration, as in the cases of Dresden and Hiroshima.

*   *   *

The "professional" soldier had always preferred the short campaign and war, with a minimum of casualties on both sides and enough glory to share afterward. After August 1776, however, warfare would no longer be a question of one prince contesting the title to a piece of land with another, while a few soldiers sought honor, booty and adventure, and others, the vast majority, along with local residents, tried to make the best of a difficult but not impossible situation. No longer would there be gentlemanly contests, outmaneuvering or successful sieges with both sides coming to basically reasonable solutions — one side agreeing to lose and the winner granting generous conditions of surrender. Generosity, it was agreed at the time, reduced rancor and removed to a degree, vengeance as a cause for a following war.* Unconditional surrender only grew to become the goal in future wars filled with continued mutual massacre and devastation until the weaker side's absolute capitulation.

---

*In the American Revolution terms of surrender were on occasion not honored. The most famous case was that of the so-called "Convention Army." When Burgoyne lost at Saratoga to Generals Arnold and Gates, he negotiated parole for his army and safe conduct to Boston, where it would take ship to England under the promise of never fighting again in the war. Aside from Burgoyne and a few others, however, none of these men were released. A powerful faction in the Continental Congress argued that 5,000 men returned to England, even if they were not to fight again, would release another 5,000 to add to the British forces in America. For the rest of the war, the "Convention Army" of prisoners was marched from upstate New York, through Massachusetts, to Virginia and back into Pennsylvania, with the hope that there would be deserters, as there were when the Hessians passed through Pennsylvania Dutch country. After five years of wandering, often at the point of starvation with basic necessities unsupplied, only about 2,300 eventually returned home.

With the American Revolution, the status of Clausewitz's third participant in war—the people—changed. Under the 18th-century autocratic governments of Europe, the people were in theory ruled paternally. They were, for the most part, untroubled by warfare, which was a matter for kings and their armies.

Over the centuries, various groups within the emerging nations had gained a variety of privileges and duties. The nobility, through feudal allegiances, secured its place at the top—in the military, the officer class— with special treatment in legal matters and, often, in the limited or complete avoidance of taxation. The religious establishments, Protestant and Catholic alike, had their own special privileges, primarily in quasi-legal independence and general exemption from taxation. The middle classes, who paid the greatest part of the taxes, had developed into countless groupings, primarily municipal, guild, trade and fraternal organizations, each with its special freedoms and social obligations negotiated with the monarchy or the ruling nobles.

The working classes, at the bottom of the social ladder, bore the heaviest burdens of the state: taxation, if they had anything worth taxing, tithes to the church whether they belonged to the state's official religion or not and, last, the corvée: labor owed to their lord, and, through him, to their monarch. And, for the military forces, while gentlemen, or those who looked like gentlemen, were exempt, workers and peasants were subject to impressment.

Things were less severe in the American colonies, where there was scarcely any nobility. People had the freedom to move west to seek a new life and had greater mobility, both in social and economic terms, than in Europe.

But many of the oppressive practices of the Old World weighed on the Americans. The 17th- and 18th-century mercantile system and its Navigation Acts hindered the development of manufacturing other than for local use. And taxation, no matter how light by today's standards, without representation, galled the colonists. It was voted on by a Parliament that gave only the slightest consideration to the people in the colonies. The Americans considered themselves British and were seeking the same rights as the British at home enjoyed.

In the view of many thinkers and social activists of the 18th century's

Age of Enlightenment, the autocratic system did not work as well as it should. At the top there was both an unwillingness to share privileges and the constant attempt to secure more. At the bottom, the people who had no say in their government were asked, it was perceived at the time, to contribute growing percentages of their labor and whatever they earned. Resentment grew over such injustices and over the corruption of the upper classes and the government. This corruption may have been no greater than it is today, but it was more blatant. The people believed they could do little, if anything, about it.

In the latter part of the century, grievances were at the flash point—particularly in America, where the vested institutions of the Old World had less hold and were unable to act as moderating forces. The American colonists had already begun to taste freedoms denied them elsewhere. A number of actions by Parliament, foolish, in retrospect, tilted the balance and even petitions to the King went unanswered. With the Declaration of Independence came true freedom—*if* the Americans could hold on to it in the face of British reaction.

*   *   *

Because of the intricate feudal system in Europe and because of economic realities, the burden of serving in the armies was essentially born by two equally useless classes. The officer corps—except in some of the technical services, artillery and engineers—was filled by excess members of the nobility, the younger sons who would not inherit the family lands and could not go into business. The middle class, who worked and paid taxes, were too valuable to serve in the ranks, so the common soldier was usually recruited from the lowest members of society, the unemployed, the otherwise idle and those in prison.

In a democracy, on the other hand, *everyone* would be expected to pull his weight. In theory this meant equality before the law, equality of opportunity and equality in taxation and military service. In the American colonies at the time one could see the early strivings of this duality of liberty and responsibility, although, as in any transition, some of the old existed along with the new.

Fifteen years later, in the fertile political soil of France, these seeds would again blossom. The French Revolutionary thinkers had refined and organized the thoughts put forward on both sides of the Atlantic during the previous two generations. The motto of the new French government was *"Liberté, Egalité, Fraternité."* Liberty freed men from earlier restrictions and gave them opportunity to be whatever they could be. Equality did away with social privileges; every man was equal before the law. Fraternity, however, though expressing the idea of a universal brotherhood of man, became instead, fervent nationalism. Collectively, these principles meant that in exchange for an infinitessimal share of sovereignty — the vote — the new citizens to a man were expected to work and fight for the greater glory of France and the Revolution.*

In the beginning, mass levies of French conscripts were fighting the reactionary armies of those other European powers seeking to restore the monarchy. When the French had stabilized their borders, the idea of universal brotherhood then developed into a missionary zeal to convert the rest of Europe to the new system, toppling by force of arms the old dynastic organizations. Aside from the assumed joy the French revolutionaries would share by spreading their idea of democracy, its acceptance by "oppressed" peoples across Europe would help assuage doubts over the propriety of the methods used. Regicide, the Reign of Terror and the brutal exterminations of uncooperating parts of the French population were seen as necessary sacrifices on the altar of liberty.

With all the military exemptions of the Old Regime lifted and with every man expected to serve, an ocean of manpower was released. The French could field armies of hundreds of thousands. With such greater numbers in this type of warfare, life was cheap; losses of men did not matter for there was always a new crop of eighteen-year-olds. From 1792 to 1800 the French lost 700,000 from a population of 36 million. During Napoleon's ill-advised ventures in Spain and Russia the average doubled and tripled. (Napoleon, it is recalled, said he could afford to lose 30,000 men a month.)

---

*Some of the fighting was required to suppress the revolt in the French colony of Haiti, where the slaves were seeking their own freedom from the French. Since Haiti was so important to the French trade balance at the time, however, this struggle could be considered "nationalistic" on the part of the French, thus keeping within the bounds of their revolutionary agenda: A Jacobin pamphlet of 1794 stated, "The uprising of the blacks in Haiti is a true Vendée."

At the same time, the French Revolution temporarily swept away many of the old institutions and privileges, as well as those laws and customs that had greatly limited the taxing powers of 18th-century Europe. With this obliteration of institutions, families were allowed to sell their properties and permitted the free exchange of money that had been curtailed under the guilds and other corporate entities. In effect, the French Revolution established for a time the triumph of capitalism. The free flow of money made the French Government suddenly rich. With universal taxation and universal work to spread its ideas, France could afford its massive armies and their concomitant losses. In the end, revolutionary France found itself fighting aggressive wars under the leadership of an emperor, resembling a totalitarian state more than a democracy.

The earlier American Revolution was far less drastic and the Continental Congress had the same type of troubles supporting the war as any European king might have had. The individual colonies, which separated the new American central government from its citizens, interfered with obtaining money and manpower for the war of liberation. The Continental Congress had to request funds and men from the sovereign colonies, which might or might not comply, or only contribute in part, holding on to their resources for local needs.

* * *

"Democratic warfare" involves the total effort of a people and its government, with all the resources of the state devoted to the absolute destruction of the enemy. It is characterized by the absolute certainty that one's side is completely in the right, and that the other side not only started the war—for reasons apparent, or better still, for no apparent reason, which shows the enemy in its truly fiendish light—but that the other side is both totally wrong and completely lacking in human values and qualities. Often this national fervor is genuine, at the beginning of a conflict. However, as democratic warfare tends to be a long-drawn-out affair, bellicose feelings can fade—particularly as the costs in people and money (often borrowed) begin to tell. To maintain the high level of commitment required, governments sooner or later rely on "committees of safety," political commissars, and police action to weed out dissenters, slackers and the generally disillusioned and disaffected.

The more visible side of this psychological war effort to strengthen the morale of a people is reflected by the often voluntary, but sometimes coerced, contributions of the media, which include speakers at various public forums ranging from the street corner to the pulpit. Passion is useful in promoting morale in times of adversity, especially when the war begins to hit home. When passion is raised to a madness and used for vengeance, it becomes a military and political liability, leading to wasted effort on one hand and atrocities on the other.

Because of the extent of commitment in a democratic war, the winner is inclined to demand unconditional surrender and usually attempts to exact exorbitant reparations. He may seek, too, geographical dismemberment of the loser. To avoid such a debacle, the other side must draw on all its resources in turn. After the mutual exhaustion, one side wins. But human beings are resilient. In a generation or so, the losers are ready to seek revenge, as recent events have shown.

In the 18th century, the rules of warfare kept destruction in bounds and away from the general population, for the most part. Objectives were specific and peace terms, if not amicable, at least did not result in what could be called a maniacal desire for revenge. "Democratic warfare," it seems, can end up being quite different.

The first battle of all the "democratic wars" was the Battle of Brooklyn. The British won the battle. But even though the winners had been successful in putting down an earlier war of national liberation— but one which was not necessarily a patriotic war, the Jacobite Rebellion*— they were unable to successfully prosecute the American affair and, seven years later, retired from the field.

After the time of the Revolution, whole continents would be drenched in the blood of patriots, as well as that of an ever-growing number of bystanders. As the American Revolution signaled the passing of the old order, the Battle of Brooklyn heralded the red dawn to come.

---

*While the Jacobite Rebellion (1745–46) was an effort to return the House of Stewart to the throne in the person of the "Young Pretender," Bonnie Prince Charlie, it was viewed as a war of national liberation in Scotland. The average Scots soldier, however, was still following his lord into battle, a condition more feudal than democratic in nature.

CHAPTER I

"A kind of key to the whole continent"

IT WAS FIFTEEN MONTHS from the time hostilities broke out at the battles of Lexington and Concord, April 19, 1775, to the acceptance by the colonies of the Declaration of Independence in July 1776. And for these fifteen months, New York City lay under the threat of British invasion.

In the early days of the rebellion, military action had taken place primarily in Massachusetts. The British had tried to smash the uprising in the spring of 1775, winning the field, albeit with excessive casualties, in the battle at Bunker Hill and Breed's Hill. However, constant and increasing pressure from the Americans entrenched on the heights surrounding Boston forced the British into an ever more defensive stance. The growing American army and the arrival of scores of cannon taken from Fort Ticonderoga in New York convinced General Howe, in command at Boston, that his position there would be untenable. He evacuated the city on March 17, 1776.

Despite the setback in Boston, the British hoped to end the war in a battle in which they could bring to bear an overwhelming force. General William Howe described this as "a decisive Action, than which nothing is more to be desired or sought for by us as the most effectual Means to terminate this expensive War."[1]

In the geopolitical scheme of things, New York was the most important strategic position to occupy. Early in 1776 John Adams called

13

it "a kind of key to the whole continent."[2] Besides even then comprising the largest metropolitan area in America, the port city formed the hub of multiple trade routes stemming inland — bonuses for any invader. Washington wrote to the Continental Congress: "Should they [the British] gain that Town and the Command of the North [Hudson] River, they can stop the intercourse between the northern and southern Colonies, upon which depends the Safety of America."[3] As well as commanding the major north–south routes from New England to the other colonies, the Hudson and Mohawk valleys were the prime routes to Canada and the northwest. Seizing New York would divide the colonies as well as provide a strong and easily accessed base of operations on Long Island, should there be any mopping up to do.

The British believed they would face a weak and disorganized army in New York and a population more Loyalist, or at least more neutral, than that of New England. Certainly, the British reasoned, the opposition would be less firm and led by less rabid leaders than were the Minutemen around Boston. The New York provincial militia, for instance, was inexperienced and pitifully equipped. Its organizational structure and concept of warfare could be called, in charity, "primitive," in many cases not easily distinguishable from that of a band of Neanderthal hunters. Just as American ardor for independence was considered in many locales to be half-hearted at best, reports from political agents (read: agents in place, or spies) showed considerable support for the British in Westchester, Staten Island and western Long Island, if not in New York itself.

The British were not lacking in confidence for the outcome of any military action they might take. One experienced "America hand," Major General James Grant, who had served well in the French and Indian War and was to figure prominently in the Battle of Brooklyn, stood up in Parliament and declared that with 5,000 British regulars he could march from one end of the continent to the other. This boast was overheard by William Alexander of New Jersey, who was in London to secure his claim to the title of the Scottish earldom of Stirling. He was later to repeat Grant's statement to the Maryland troops on the morning of the Battle of Brooklyn, when they were about to face Grant's men.

According to the British plan, after taking New York, a large force would march north along the Hudson to meet a 10,000-man strong column moving south from Canada commanded by Major General Sir Guy Carleton. Thus cut off, New England would then be isolated from the rest of the colonies and at the mercy of the British. On paper the plan was admirable; in practice, it left much to be desired. The forces in Canada and those to invade New York were regarded in London as separate armies, and thus lacked a unified command. In addition, no senior British commander had more than a limited knowledge of the terrain outside of New York City. And in London, the vagaries of weather conditions, both on a continent three thousand miles away, and at sea, were given little thought. Finally, as subsequent events in the Revolution would prove, the British were seldom able to move freely inland, and were only able to husband their superiority when they stayed close to the ports (and the Royal Navy).

Once Long Island and the port of New York had been secured, went the plan, a base would be established in Rhode Island for punitive raids on New England as far north as Maine. New York and Rhode Island would serve as bases for a tight blockade of the coast.

The British invasion of New York would be led by the Howe brothers, general and admiral, sons of Viscount Howe of the Irish peerage.

General Sir William Howe (1729–1814) served under General Wolfe at the Battle of Quebec and in fact had led the small party of light infantry that discovered the path leading up to the Plains of Abraham in that battle. Wolfe, who died at Quebec, had written: "No officer had a more brilliant record of service"[4] than Howe. Made Major General in 1772, Howe was entrusted with training a number of companies from line regiments in the new system of drill that was intended to counter the irregular warfare anticipated in the colonies. Howe succeeded General Thomas Gage in 1775 as commander-in-chief of the British forces in America. Though he was eventually superseded in 1778 by Sir Henry Clinton after failing to destroy the Americans at Valley Forge, his lifetime record in battles was flawless — although one, viewed in official circles as a small action, did come at a heavy price in casualties: Bunker Hill.

General Howe's older brother, Admiral Lord Richard Howe (1726–99), left Eton at thirteen to join the Navy, seeing action under Rear Admiral George Anson against the Spanish in the Pacific. Made captain at the age of twenty, he distinguished himself in the Seven Years' War.

Known throughout the fleet as "Black Dick," he was to prove himself one of the greatest admirals in the British Navy. He succeeded to the title of Earl after the death of his brother, Brigadier General George Howe, who was killed at Fort Ticonderoga in 1758, and became commander of the fleet in America after serving for a time as Treasurer of the Navy.

Despite (or because of) the Howe family's extensive combat experience, the brothers were flexible toward the idea of a negotiated settlement and were, in fact, also empowered as peace commissioners. Although their initial attempts to communicate with General Washington were spurned, the brothers waited two weeks after the Battle of Brooklyn in order to arrange (fruitless) peace talks. They would wait another week following the breakoff of these talks to follow up militarily, during which time Washington would regroup and fortify upper Manhattan.

In any case, the original British plan for a two-pronged advance in 1776 did not approach success. General Carleton never advanced beyond Lake Champlain. A later attempt on a similar theme resulted in General Burgoyne's disastrous defeat at Saratoga in upstate New York. Clearly, the best hopes of the British lay in seizing New York City with a sudden, massive blow, thereby destroying the main American forces that were assembled there.

*   *   *

For over a year, the "shot heard 'round the world" echoed with mixed reverberations in the environs of New York City. The Royal Governor of New York Province, William Tryon, remained in office; the Royal Courts and administration were still in existence. British warships were at anchor in the harbor. The residents, be they Loyalist Tories or revolutionary Whigs, feared these ships would bombard the city and set it on fire should there be sufficient provocation. Twenty thousand or so free inhabitants of Manhattan, and about three thousand slaves, lived closely packed in some 4,000 houses, mostly made of wood, from the Battery (named after its artillery emplacement) to just below today's City Hall Park.

The political climate, to be sure, was that of rebellion. New York had even been called the "Cock Pit of the Revolution."[5] For the previous two years there had been two parallel governments in the province: the Royal administration, with its Assembly, which seldom met; and the revolutionary Provincial Congress, which held its meetings in a room at City Hall, on Wall Street. This room was just down the hall from where its Royal equivalent would have sat were it in session.

Tryon, who would have much rather have been in command of a battalion in the British Army, had accepted his appointment with reluctance. He was prone to moderation, if at all possible, hoping for a reconciliation with the disaffected citizens of the province. This quest for moderation was tested when his ship arrived from England and anchored off Manhattan Island. It seems that both he, the newly appointed Royal Governor, and the newly commissioned commander-in-chief of the Continental forces, George Washington, en route from Philadelphia to join the army laying siege to Boston, arrived on the same day, Sunday, June 25, 1775.

Most residents of New York wanted to welcome both, to show variously their allegiance and/or present their petitions and grievances to whomever would be in a position, sooner or later, to help. And certainly they did not want either of the two leaders to take offense. But the notables on shore had a problem. There were only ten companies of militia, just enough to provide one parade at a time. The community leaders could not greet both officials should they land simultaneously.

Tryon tactfully eased their difficulties by letting it be known that matters of state kept him from landing until 8 P.M. Greatly relieved, the New Yorkers meanwhile greeted General Washington at a ferry slip uptown, held a parade of honor and fêted him at an early welcoming dinner.

Shortly before 8 o'clock, the commandant of the militia, Colonel John Lasher, formed up the companies of his Independent Battalion at the Battery, where Tryon was due to land. Various prominent citizens slipped away from the Washington dinner and made their way downtown, arriving as the barge of the Royal Governor approached the shore. Tryon was then given a formal escort to the house of Philip Livingstone, one which the Governor had rented, the official residence having recently been burned to the ground, cause unknown. There he held a reception, greeting Tories and Whigs alike, and heard, although somewhat rephrased, the same sentiments and concerns expressed at the earlier dinner.

From the start, his position was ambivalent. After mounting difficulties, on October 13, 1775, Tryon sent to safe places as many of his official records as he could collect. The current ones he kept with him, while those less immediately needed began a long journey, first to Governors Island, then to the home of a Loyalist on Long Island.* As for Tryon himself, he wrote to the Earl of Dartmouth on October 16th: "The City has been in continual agitation and ferment encreased (*sic*) by a recommendation and resolve of the Continental Congress that this provincial Congress should take into consideration the expedience of seizing or securing the Crown Officers. . . . I kept out of Town all Thursday at the Governor's Island and in the evening the *Asia* boat landed me at Long Island and [I] lay at Mr. Astell's (*sic*) at Flatbush."[6]

Tryon's wanderings took him later that month to the liner *Duchess of Gordon*, riding at anchor in the North River, as that mile-long section of the Hudson which runs due north and south was called. On board he remained, until after the battle, as Royal Governor in a sort of political limbo.

No matter how conciliatory Tryon may have been, his position as well as that of the opposition was irrevocably altered at the end of 1775, when Parliament passed the Prohibitory Acts declaring that a state of war existed between Britain and her rebellious colonies.

Up to this point, the protestors in America had been seeking the rights they firmly believed they should have enjoyed as Englishmen under Parliament and which were supposed to have been protected by the Monarch. The action of Parliament swelled the ranks of the rebels with those who had been wavering and hoping for a reconciliation. Now it would only be a matter of months before the Declaration of Independence — addressed to George III — would be issued.

* * *

On a more local level, the difficulties proposed by the duality of government in New York were settled, to a degree, on February 1, 1776, when fifteen members of the rebellious Provincial Congress managed to be elected to the Royal Assembly, the voters choosing the entire

---

*These records, as well as others from the time of the British occupation, have disappeared. Historians speculate they may be gathering dust in some warehouse or cellar in England.

anti-Tory slate. Thus, problems resulting from other aspects of the process of revolution could now be solved with legal nicety by having a majority of duly elected representatives of the American cause in the opponent's lawmaking body—that is, if it ever met.

On the streets, the revolution showed its darker side: the *mobile vulgus,* the mob. There were growing numbers of assaults on Tories, with the usual settlement of personal grievances by these mobs, the self-proclaimed "Sons of Liberty." Such groups in New York City may have professed the same beliefs as those similarly named bodies elsewhere in the colonies, but their way of applying these beliefs differed greatly.

In New York City, these patriotic societies were made up of workers, street idlers and miscellaneous patrons of the taverns in which they convened. Although younger members of prominent families sought to control—and even claimed to control—these mobs, they were led in practice by those who would be called "ward heelers" at a later date: mostly artisans, shop owners and barkeepers active in local politics. Neither the leaders nor the members of these ad hoc committees were overly troubled by respect for due process of the law. In their contribution to the cause, they preferred tarring and rail-riding to other, less physical responses to the Tory menace.

As the number of American soldiers increased in New York, the mobs became bolder. One Peter Elting wrote: "We had some grand Tory rides in this city this week. . . . Several of them were handled very roughly, being carried through the streets on rails, their clothes tore from their backs and their bodies pretty well mingled with the dust. . . . There is hardly a Tory face to be seen this morning."[7]

Finding more attractive the practices of rioting, looting and intimidation—the core of the action of these mobs—they were less prone to actual constructive work. At the reading of the Declaration of Independence on July 9, 1776—the day the colony of New York ratified it—the monumental equestrian statue of George III was pulled down and broken up to mold bullets for the patriots' cause. Freedom-loving though New York's members of the Sons of Liberty were, most of those doing the actual work during this event were the black slaves of some of the more affluent members.

The Tory menace was also a concern at the level of the Provincial

Congress. In mid-September it decided to penalize those residents who had not signed the so-called General Association. This was a document whose signers agreed to "associate under all the ties of religion, honor and love of our country to adopt. . .whatever measures may be recommended by the Continental Congress resolved upon by the Provincial Congress for the purpose of preserving our constitution. . ." Nonsigners were to be disarmed: ". . .all such arms as are fit for the use of the troops raised in this colony, which shall be found in the hands of any person who has not signed the General Association, shall be impressed for the use of such troops,"[8] read the Provincial Congress' decree.

Attempts to collect weapons were met with stiff resistance in Queens County. "The people [of Queens]," one Whig reported, "conceal all their arms that are of any value; many declare that they know nothing about the Congress, nor do they care anything for the orders of Congress, and say that they would sooner or later lose their lives than give up their arms; and that they would blow out any man's brains who would attempt to take them."[9] This resistance was not just on the part of individuals; most of it was organized. Responding to this Whig's additional observation that it would take a militia battalion to collect the weapons, Richard Hewlett, who had raised and armed a Loyalist company in Hempstead, said: "Had your battalion appeared, we would have warmed their sides."[10]

In addition to arms-collecting activities, the Committee of Safety of the Provincial Congress was active in getting those holding principles "inimical" to its views to swear, if not loyalty to the American cause, at least non-support of the British. As the months wore on, and the threat of invasion grew, the zealots in the provincial body, with the active help of General Charles Henry Lee and the soldiers under his command, extended this "swearing" beyond the "inimicals" to the "equivocals"— those who didn't care either way. Many suspected Loyalists were thus compelled to swear more than once, and in some cases, post bond for good behavior.

This Tory hunt, however, was flawed from the beginning. No one had really formed a good description of what was "inimical." The order issued by the Continental Congress on October 9, 1775, to arrest any who might "endanger the safety of the colonies if left at large"[11] was too vague to help the Committee of Safety sort out friends from potential foes on the home front.

Also, the Committee's methodology was flawed. The lists of suspects had been made up from the election rolls and overlooked the majority of the population, who were not men of property and therefore could not vote. Women, even widows, who could own property at that time, were not even considered, although many were to prove helpful to the Tory cause.

Meanwhile, those colonists who were actually stockpiling arms and/or recruiting potential volunteers for Loyalist units should the fighting begin — and supplying information to the British governor — had either gone underground or were little troubled over swearing oaths to a cause they believed treasonous. Any oath sworn at the point of a gun, or in the face of a potential house-burning, Tories believed, with good logic and theology on their side, was not valid.*

In January 1776, the Continental Congress stepped up its efforts against the Loyalists, declaring non-signers to be in contempt of Congress and therefore outside the law. As the English presence in the colony of New York was now greatly diminished, Loyalists had no legal recourse at all. That month, Colonel Nathaniel Heard arrived from New Jersey with several hundred militiamen and 300 troops from the Connecticut Line; he had orders to continue disarming Loyalists and arrest their leaders.

These leaders, when caught, were sent to Philadelphia for questioning by the Congress. Loyalists who had voted in a recent election for the Queens delegation to Congress (at that time the secret ballot was viewed as the handmaiden to conspiracy, and names and their votes had been recorded) lost their civil rights. They were to be boycotted, trade and contact with them condemned and they could not travel without permission. The boycott was to be total, but, at least in legal matters, balanced. Lawyers were prohibited either from defending them or prosecuting them.

---

*The British, during their occupation of Long Island, also subscribed to the technique of "loyalty swearing." However, as Captain John Bowater, Royal Marines, wrote to Admiral Howe, the American Loyalists on Long Island "swallow the oaths of allegiance to the King and [American] Congress with as much ease as your Lordship does poached eggs."[12]

While all this tumult was going on ashore, Tryon was safely afloat, receiving guests by day and messages on the situation from Loyalists who rowed to his ship with muffled oars at night. Fearing to provoke him—for a red-hot shot from even one British ship could incinerate the town— the Provincial Congress ordered his ship and any other British ship in port to be regularly supplied. Only in the few weeks approaching the battle did the Continentals limit the visitors Tryon could receive, in an attempt to keep him in the dark about American preparations.

Tryon had shown moderation and tact, and later extreme prudence, in the face of the growing American threat. He could do little but live aboard his ship and wait.

The Royal Governor's position may have been a strange one, but that of the two commanders of the British forces marshaled to end the rebellion by one means or another was downright peculiar, and might even have contributed to the eventual loss of the war. In addition to being military commanders, with the initial mandate to crush the rebellion in one swift blow, they were also empowered as Royal Peace Commissioners. On May 6, 1776, "letters patent under the great seal" had been issued, naming the two special commissioners "for granting pardons and taking other measures for the conciliation of the Colonies."[13] Their status as military commanders was further compromised by their reputation as leaders among the anti-war opposition in Parliament, for having spoken out vigorously against the war and for not being known to have changed their minds.

These two men, Admiral Lord Richard Howe and his brother, General Sir William, had obviously been chosen for their military abilities rather than their politics. Lord Richard was a prominent Whig and among his colleagues in the House of Lords was well known for his opposition to the war in the colonies. In fact, he had held secret meetings with Benjamin Franklin during the winter of 1774–75 in an effort to resolve difficulties between the colonies and England. At that time Franklin was the "agent"—a post we would describe as that of a lobbyist— for the colonies of Georgia, Massachusetts, New Jersey and Pennsylvania. Sir William was a leading Whig in the House of Commons, and as opposed as his brother to any expansion of the conflict.

In July 1776, while the largest invasion force the British had yet mounted was arriving in Staten Island, the two Howes issued a "Declaration," via Tory sympathizers, to be posted in towns in the region. This widely distributed document granted "a free and general pardon to all who in the tumult and disorder of the times may have deviated from just allegiance, and are willing by a speedy return to their duty to reap the benefits of the royal favor."[14]

With the July 9th reading of the Declaration of Independence to the American troops, however, it was no longer a case of the colonists' fighting for their rights as Englishmen. Now, they were fighting for independence from England and liberty to choose their own form of government. The great patriotic army had received its mandate.

CHAPTER II

"Kindness and real abundance is everywhere"

T HE PORT OF NEW YORK is an hourglass-shaped bay, running north to south with its entrance from the Atlantic to the east. On the west is New Jersey with numerous rivers, and Staten Island. Sandy Hook, New Jersey, was the first landfall for ships approaching the port. Coney Island, called Ile des Lapins on early French maps and the only place the original Dutch settlers found rabbits—"coneys" in Old English—was the other gatepost of the harbor.

In the early days of navigation, before channels were marked and lighthouses established, the passage across the bar—the bulging deposit of silt washed down the Hudson River that formed a barrier across the entrance to the harbor just below the surface—could be an exquisite piece of navigation for a large ship. Sloops and some smaller frigates could slip across the bar at high tide. The deep-draft ships of the line and transports—often called "liners" in the 18th century—had to use harbor pilots who knew where the shifting channels were. Or, the captain of a large ship could proceed very slowly and in careful control of his vessel—an interesting proposition in the age of wind-powered navigation—following one of his small boats from which a sailor would cast a lead weight on the end of a line to search out the channel.

The bar was known as the graveyard of ships. In storms, one caught on the bar could easily tear itself apart, or without navigational aids it could mistakenly be sailed directly onto the shore.

In 1761 and 1762 the Royal Colonial Assembly of New York raised money for a lighthouse on Sandy Hook through two lotteries and a tax on the tonnage of ships entering the harbor. The 103-foot-tall structure could be seen at about 15 miles from the deck of a man-of-war and 30 miles from its topgallant yard.

In March 1776, the lamps and oil were removed to thwart a British fleet's entering the port. But as in any professional military operation, the British sent a frigate to reconnoiter. It landed a party of Royal Marines and sailors to secure the lighthouse and restore it to operation. Before the arrival of the rest of the British armada, sent to crush the rebellion, an attack by local militia on June 1st was beaten off and what damage they had caused easily repaired.

The entry to the Upper Bay was through the Narrows, a channel about a mile wide. Overlooking the Narrows were heights where, for later wars, Forts Hamilton and Wadsworth were built. The Upper Bay, six miles north to south and about four miles east to west, was bordered on the west by Staten Island, an irregular pentagon in shape, measuring 13 by seven miles and completely surrounded by waters navigable by the ships of the British Navy. Separating this island from New Jersey was the Kill Van Kull and (farther south) the Arthur Kill—"kill" being the Dutch word for channel or creek.

To the north lay the Hudson River, the southern tip of Manhattan Island and an estuary named the East River. Both the Upper and Lower Bays were bounded on the east by Kings County—what is today the Borough of Brooklyn. The most sheltered anchorage for a large number of ships was off the town of Saint George on the north shore of Staten Island. In the upper bay were a number of islands, one of which, Governors, about a third of the way from Brooklyn to New York City, was fortified with guns to complement the artillery positions on Brooklyn Heights and in the Battery* at the tip of Manhattan Island.

Today's New York County—the Borough of Manhattan—is an island, one and a half miles at its widest point in 1776, which runs some

---

*It was called the Grand Battery at the time. This government compound was anchored on the west, where the Customs House is now, by Fort George, the colony's main arsenal, and on the east, earlier, by Whitehall, the governor's official residence.

12 miles in a northeasterly direction. It is separated from neighboring New Jersey by the one-and-a-half-mile-wide Hudson River. To Manhattan's north is the Harlem Creek (enlarged to the status of river in the late 19th century), fordable in 1776 on horseback when the tide was low and usable by shallow draft boats when the tide was running. The Harlem is the border between Manhattan and Westchester County, which in 1776 included today's Borough of the Bronx.

To the east, the one-mile-wide East River separates Manhattan and the Bronx from Long Island. In British navigation advice at the time of the Battle of Brooklyn, the East River was described as very tricky, with treacherous tides, particularly near the entry of the Harlem Creek at about halfway along the estuary's 12-mile stretch, a place called Hellgate.* Ships were advised only to attempt the passage in the best of weather and, then, only when exercising extreme caution.

The tides that enter New York Bay from the south push up the East River. They also race up the Hudson on a 15-mile journey to re-enter the East River via the Harlem. Further compounding the difficulties of sailing on the East River is the tide that sweeps into Long Island Sound from the Atlantic. It picks up force as it travels the funnel-shaped Sound to pour into the East River at its northern extremity at Whitestone, a mile or so north of the old town of Flushing. All these tides meet at Hellgate, a tidal raceway one-quarter of a mile wide.

So dangerous was Hellgate in the age of sail that any successful passage by a large ship was the news of the town. A German, Major Baurmeister, who was in the British army of occupation, commented:

> . . .very dangerous and dreadful strait or passage, called *Hell-Gates,* between the East River and the Sound; where the two tides meeting cause a horrible whirlpool, the vortex of which is called the Pot, and drawing in and swallowing up every thing that approaches near it, dashes them to pieces upon the rocks upon

---

Hellgat, in Dutch. The name comes from Indian legends recorded by Dutch settlers to indicate a maritime entrance to the netherworld. To a small-boat operator, the description by Washington Irving in *A History of New York* is more truth than hyperbole: "For now the late dimpling current began to brawl around them and the waves to boil and foam with horrific fury."

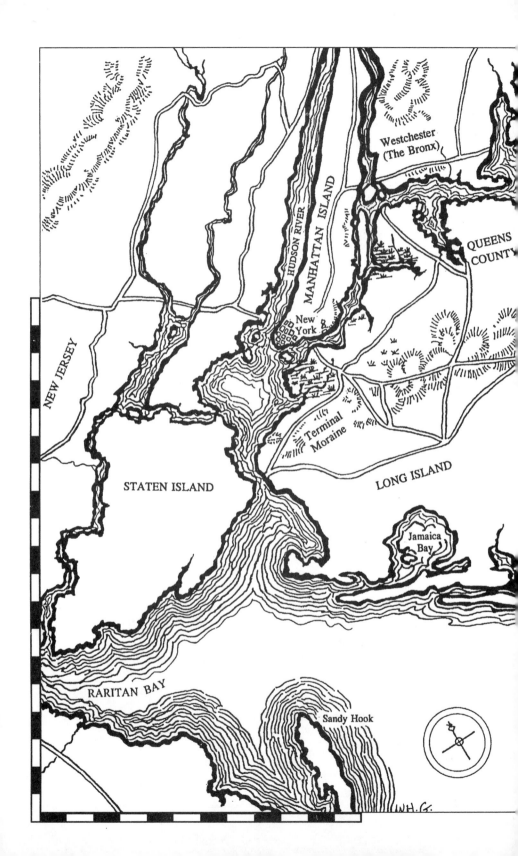

NEW JERSEY

Westchester
(The Bronx)

QUEENS
COUNTY

HUDSON RIVER

MANHATTAN ISLAND

New
York

Terminal
Moraine

STATEN ISLAND

LONG ISLAND

Jamaica
Bay

RARITAN BAY

Sandy Hook

W.H.G.

the bottom. . . . Before the late war, a top-sail vessel was seldom ever known to pass through Hell-Gates; but since the commencement of it, fleets of transports with frigates for their convoy, have frequently ventured and accomplished it; the *Niger,* indeed, a very fine frigate of thirty-two guns, generally struck on some hidden rock, every time she attempted this passage. But what is still more extraordinary, that daring veteran, Sir James Wallace, to the astonishment of every person who ever saw or heard of it, carried His Majesty's ship, the *Experiment,* of fifty guns, safe through Hell-Gates, from the east end of the Sound to New York; when the French fleet under D'Estaing lay off Sandy Hook, and blocked up the harbor and city of New York, some ships of the line being also sent by D'Estaing round the east end of Long Island to cruise in the Sound for the same purpose, so that the *Experiment* must inevitably have fallen into their hands, had it not been for this bold and successful attempt of her gallant commander.[1]

By the 1850s, in the early age of steam navigation, the United States Army Corps of Engineers estimated that about 1,000 ships ran aground each year in the passage, a moderate number of them sinking. The Corps decided to clear the channel of these rocks, which were once, in Indian legends, called the Devil's Stepping Stones. In 1885 the Corps began to blast out the rocks against which shipping was driven by the tides and winds that compounded on one another in the narrow passage. One of the blasts was the largest man-made explosion up to that time.

* * *

Across the East River from New York lies Long Island. To the north, it is separated from Westchester and Connecticut by Long Island Sound. To the south, it faces the Atlantic Ocean. From the 1680s to the 19th century Long Island was divided into three counties: Kings, Queens (which extended about 30 miles eastward and included today's Nassau County) and Suffolk.

Twenty miles at its widest and about 130 miles long, it was populated at its western end by the Dutch—four or five generations removed from the original settlers of the colony of New Netherlands, and indifferent at best to the politics of Revolutionary America—and on its eastern end by a mixture of Tories and Whigs. The area in the center, now known as Nassau County, was primarily Tory in sentiment except for the town of North Hempstead. This town had closer ties—religious, family and economic—to Connecticut, a few hours' sail across the Sound, than it did to New York, which was at least a day's travel over what passed for roads at the time. Suffolk County too, closer geographically to New England, was also closest in spirit to its rebellious neighbors to the north.

In the center of the island lay the Great Hempstead Plain, now the ghost of its former self. It was a true prairie, the same as those in the Midwest of the United States. In Revolutionary times it extended over 60,000 acres, nearly ten square miles, and was known for its excellent wheat crop. In the spring of 1776, some 7,000 cattle and an equal number of sheep grazed on it and in the neighboring town of Oyster Bay. Long Island, rich too in fish, game and shellfish, as well as wood, was a huge fertile granary able to support a large army indefinitely.

Running down the spine of Long Island, from Oyster Bay on the Sound to a point on the coast of Brooklyn is the terminal moraine, a giant pile of rocks left by the last glacier to visit the area, the Wisconsin, of 17,000 years ago. As with all glaciers, when it advanced it carried with it rocky debris that was dropped like a conveyor belt as it stagnated, forming the arc of hills extending northeastward from the Upper Bay at about 69th Street in Bay Ridge in Brooklyn and swinging north above Jamaica at the western edge of the Great Hempstead Plain. It formed a formidable natural barrier, to be used by the American forces in the battle to come as their outer defenses, protecting the landward approaches to the harbor forts on Brooklyn Neck.

This ridge, as was three-quarters of Kings County, was covered with stands of oak, ash, chestnut, pepperidge, liquid amber (sour and sweet gum) and tulip trees, broken here and there by close-set orchards and open patches called "English meadows," which had been cleared for garden farming. Under the trees, the surface was thickly covered with brush that formed dense walls along the rutted paths serving to connect the settlements. The ridge, sometimes known as Prospect Range, was called at the time both Brookland Heights and the Heights of Guan, or Guian. Gowane, to cite another spelling, was an Indian who lived on the lowlands and next to the creek below Red Hook which was also named after him, today's Gowanus.

*   *   *

From its inception as the Village of New Amsterdam, the town and later city of New York on Manhattan Island had been a trading post, depending for sustenance on the farm produce of neighboring communities, particularly the abundance of Brooklyn, only a mile across the river at its nearest point.

Brooklyn in 1776 was a sparsely settled area of lush farmland communities, whose geographic boundaries were defined by impassable forests, marshland or rugged hills. The Hessian Colonel von Donop called Brooklyn "a beautiful island, an arcadia, a most delightful region."[2] Another Hessian, Major Baurmeister, gave a more complete description:

> The happiness of the inhabitants, whose ancestors were all Dutch, must have been great; genuine kindness and real abundance is everywhere; any thing worthless or going to ruin is nowhere to be perceived. The inhabited regions resemble the Westphalian peasant districts; upon separate farms the finest houses are built, which are planned and completed in the most elegant fashion. The furniture in them is in the best taste, nothing like which is to be seen with us, and besides as clean and neat, that altogether it surpasses every description. The female sex is universally beautiful and delicately reared, and is finely dressed in the latest European fashion, particularly in India laces, white cotton and silk gauzes; not one of these women but would consider driving a double team the easiest of work. They drive and ride out alone, having only a negro riding behind to accompany them. Near every dwelling-house negroes (their slaves) are settled who cultivate the most fertile land, pasture the cattle, and do all the menial work.[3]

Brooklyn was well known to the British. Young bucks from the Royal garrison and New York would cross the river for an evening's entertainment in and around tiny Brooklyn Village, favoring especially the old Ferry Tavern. Officers were entertained at houses in the borough or crossed Brooklyn to visit estates around the English settlements of Richmond Hill, Flushing or Jamaica in Queens County. Shooting parties were held at the extreme reaches of Brooklyn beside the marshes of Jamaica Bay or the edges of Coney Island, and hunts ranged over the fields of the New Lots, Flatlands and Flatbush. Races were regularly held, drawing festive parties of the well-to-do from New York.

Five of the six towns in what today makes up Brooklyn — Boswyck (now Bushwick); Breukelen (Brooklyn Village in downtown Brooklyn, which included Brooklyn Heights); Midwout, also called 'tVlacke-Bos (Flatbush); New Amersfort (Flatlands); and Nieuw Utrecht (New Utrecht)—were Dutch in heritage and population. The sixth town, Gravesend, while English, had been gradually assimilating itself into the general Dutch scheme of things, that of an industrious and prosperous farming district of God-fearing, family-oriented people who liked things as they were.

Gravesend had been settled in 1643 by Lady Deborah Moody, an English dissenter from the Established Church (of England). Apparently she had not been made welcome earlier by other dissenting sects, because she had been asked to leave, after England, successively, Boston, Rhode Island and Eastern Long Island, before finding a home for herself and her followers among the Dutch. (The sentiments of the residents of Gravesend in 1776, whether they were Whig or Loyalist Tory, are unknown.)

In addition to the six towns, there existed several scattered crossroads settlements; these included Greenpoint, Waal-bogt (Wallabout), Cripplebush (a mile due east of Waal-bogt), Bedford, Gowanus, and the New Lots.

These towns and settlements were connected by roads built on former Indian paths. These paths exist today, for the most part following the same routes as they did on 18th-century maps. The most important, beginning at Gravesend, was the King's Highway. It crossed Brooklyn and intersected the Jamaica Road north of today's East New York. The Jamaica Road ran east–west to connect Brooklyn Village with Jamaica and Hempstead. North–south ways included the Shore Road, which ran along the coast from Gravesend to Gowanus, and the Flatbush Road.

Then, as now, a heavily traveled route, the Flatbush Road started in the New Lots, crossed the King's Highway, and connected the most fertile lands of Brooklyn with the New York ferry at the East River. Where it passed through the hills of the terminal moraine (at today's Battle Pass) it was called, descriptively, the Valley Grove Road. At this point, the Port Road branched off to the Gowanus Creek; called the Shunpike, it was used by farmers who wanted to avoid paying the tolls on Flatbush Road. Also running north–south was the Bedford Road. Where it passed through the hills, it was called the Clove Road because it "clove through," making a pass that was an easily defensible choke point.

There were a number of crossroads taverns scattered throughout Brooklyn that were to figure in the coming battle. As well as serving beer, wine and hard spirits, and being community centers and sheltering travelers, they were also neighborhood general stores. They stocked, if modestly, goods needed on the surrounding farms. The Rising Sun Tavern, also known because of its position midway between Jamaica and Brooklyn Village as Howard's Half Way House, was at the Jamaica Pass. The Red Lion Inn was at Martense Lane and the Narrows (Shore) Road, where the first shots of the battle were fired. Valley Grove House was just north of the Flatbush Pass. And Baker's Tavern on Flatbush Road was where patriot Major General Sullivan faced his strongest British attack.

By the mid-1770s the total white population of what comprised Brooklyn was about 2,600, predominantly Dutch farmers and their families, plus some English settlers. The black population numbered as many as 1,500, including both slaves and freedmen. Whether slave or free, the blacks worked for the most part as artisans, and were used as extra hands during the planting and harvesting seasons.

By the time of the American Revolution, Brooklyn had the highest percentage of blacks to whites north of the Mason and Dixon Line. Only Charleston, South Carolina, exceeded this percentage in a near-urban seacoast area. The reason for this high percentage of blacks is hard to assess for a community that was not organized on the plantation system, however it might tie in to the ambivalent attitude of the Dutch. With the despised Spanish occupation of the Netherlands as part of their collective memory, the Dutch were considered to be significantly more

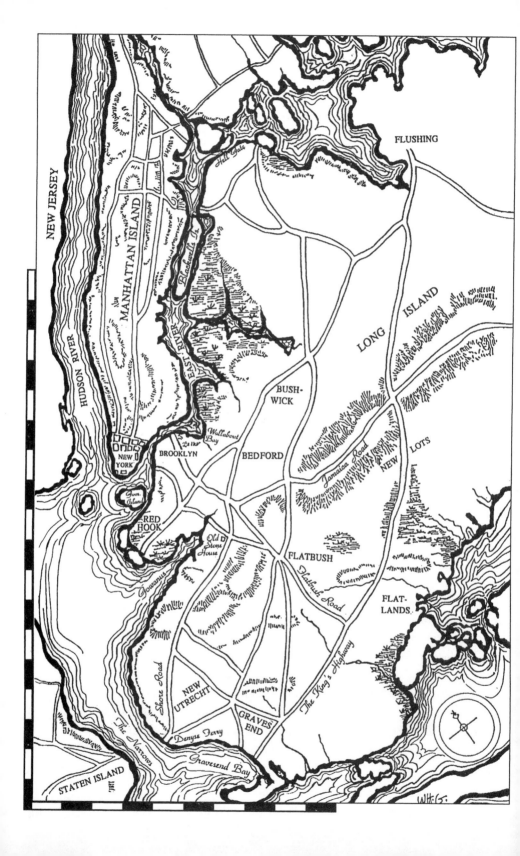

enlightened in their treatment of slaves than were their fellow English colonists. The English were scandalized, as much as they were astounded, by the liberties the Dutch farmer granted his blacks. Just as in South Africa before Apartheid, many blacks worked the fields with their Boer owners and shared the workday table. In pre-Revolutionary days, an English visitor noted: "Their blacks. . .were very free and familiar; sometimes sauntering about among the whites at meal time, with hat on head, and freely joining occasionally in conversation, as if they were one and all of the same household."[4]

In any case, whether black, English or Dutch, in one way or another the vast majority of Brooklyn's population was dependent on a relatively few large, land-holding merchant families who had extensive trading ties to Britain.

During the century of British control preceding the American Revolution, the Dutch had been left by and large to their own devices and they had prospered. Dutch was still the language of white man and black in the villages and "boueries" of Brooklyn; the Dutch Reformed Church had thrived in the Province of New Amsterdam, growing from 11 congregations when the English arrived in 1664 to 65 by 1740.

Most of the residents of Brooklyn were looked upon as apathetic Revolutionaries at best, or, at worst, hostile to any progress by either side in the coming conflict. Some, who were in favor of the American cause, prayed for a less drastic solution than war. Grace Barclay wrote: "We love this our native land, the native country of my mother, of both parents. Her [America's] course seems to us a righteous one. She is overtaxed, oppressed, insulted; my father feels this; he is indignant at it, yet. . .he hates the sin while he loves the sinner. They [the English] seem the foes of our own household to him; brother lifting up sword against brother, in unnatural warfare which he prays may speedily come to an end."[5]

In the days leading up to the British invasion in August 1776, many families packed what belongings they could and fled farther east on Long Island, only to return as winter was beginning to find homes and farmsteads devastated during the Battle of Brooklyn and the initial occupation. The contented lifestyle of the period before the Revolution was gone. Then, the Dutch of Brooklyn appeared, to Alexander Graydon, an American prisoner billeted with a farm family during the British occupation, to be "a people who seem thoroughly disposed to submit to any power that might be imposed on them."[6]

CHAPTER III

"By lies they lured them, by liquor they tempted them"

THE BRITISH FOOT SOLDIER was magnificently trained and brutally disciplined. He was, in addition, almost invariably commanded by members of the nobility or gentry whose families had enough money to buy them an officer's commission.

In today's age of democracy, civil service and merit promotions, the idea of buying a commission might seem unduly elitist. In earlier centuries, however, governments looked for two qualities in their armies: they should be reliable—able to fight wars and at the same time be uninclined to topple the government; and they should be either self-supporting or as economical as possible. (One cause of the American Revolution was the attempt by Parliament to tax the colonies for the British soldiers who were posted there.)

At the time of the American Revolution, the practice of buying commissions actually strengthened the loyalty of the officer corps fighting in America. Under other systems, officers serving with a regiment went wherever it was sent. Under the British system, those unwilling to fight former British subjects could either sell their commissions or buy into a regiment that was being sent someplace else.

In the 18th century there was no concept of military service as a citizen's duty and contribution to the welfare of the state. Indeed, while the Swiss were contemplating universal military service as one of the mechanisms of their confederation, conscription in the rebellious

American colonies was being met with greater and greater resistance.

British regiments were raised by individuals who were paid by the Crown for each soldier they could enlist and keep. Often, the recruiting followed a standard pattern: "By lies they lured them, by liquor they tempted them, and when they were dead drunk they forced a shilling into their fists."[1] Acceptance of the King's Shilling, whether consciously or not, implied a binding contract and meant a new member of the regiment. Although the recruiting officers may have had to use trickery to fill the ranks, they nonetheless sought good material. Ideally, British units were to be composed of "respectable, docile country lads, brought up by careful, thrifty parents in a decent cottage home."[2]

In the regimental structure, while subalterns bought their way into commissions and promotions, it was the non-commissioned officer, the drill sergeant and the dreaded RSM — the Regimental Sergeant Major — who provided the backbone and continuing military tradition of the unit. And it was the RSM who drilled his men until they acted by rote.

Prior to the advent of democratic nationhood, the common man had no responsibility as a citizen, with the result that, in any of the European armies' tactical formations, the average soldier was treated as an automaton, not a human being. Frederick the Great of Prussia, who strongly influenced the pattern of continental armies, believed the soldier should fear his officers — in the British Army the RSM — more than he feared the enemy. By contrast, the more independent-minded citizen soldier of the American colonies — who, while not having the vote at the time, was sure he soon would have it — was at least expected to have more tactical flexibility and show more initiative in battle.

The average British enlisted man and company-grade officer had ten years' experience. He had usually served in the same regiment during this time and was imbued with a strong corporate spirit toward his fellow soldiers. Usually, a British regiment was composed of ten companies of about 80 men each. One of the companies was of the elite grenadiers, one of the light infantry, and eight companies were soldiers of the line, who provided the mass and firepower in the traditional European-type battle.

The grenadier unit could be regarded as today's heavy-weapons company. Its men were chosen for their height. They were in the front of an advancing column and were most often used in the center of the line to carry the heaviest weight in a bayonet charge. However, as their name implies, these units were formed for other purposes, such as assaulting enemy positions with hand-thrown bombs or grenades. The idea was to run up to enemy emplacements carrying bombs with burning fuses—these having been lit at the last convenient moment with cigars—and toss them, praying they would go off only at the end of their flight and silence the opposition. Considering their manufacture, the bombs usually didn't go off—the fuses were extinguished by damp, the wind, or lack of it, or poor construction—or they went off too soon. Often the grenades contained too much powder, either by accident or by design, so their killing radius became greater than the distance they could be thrown. The practice was to throw the bomb, turn and run away from it as fast as possible, hopefully to find a nearby hole to dive into. The fur helmet, or busby, the grenadiers wore not only accented height, adding another foot to their natural six-foot-plus stature, but also acted as a primitive defense, the fur absorbing to a degree the concussion from a grenade.

In this time of the "fighting" line, most of the British units wore red coats for visibility and to impress the enemy in the smoke of battle. The color also masked blood, either from the wounded soldier, or, more importantly, blood splashed from a comrade. The red coat also gave rise to epithets, such as Lobster Backs or Bloody Backs.

(The British Rifle Regiment, formed later as a result of lessons learned in the American Revolution, wore green uniforms, as did some mounted infantry units. The color offered some degree of camouflage, at least at a distance, as these men were expected to engage in more irregular warfare, skirmishing and fighting generally in small groups. Ideally, uniforms were issued at the end of the winter; their color, which approximated spring greenery, faded as the year progressed to match the earth-toned hues of autumn.)

The light-infantry companies were skirmishers who did the reconnaissance, raided, attacked targets of opportunity and protected the flanks of an advancing column. Ironically, the light infantry was an American invention, dating from the French and Indian War, based on such units as Robert Rogers' Rangers. These were highly trained in Indian fighting, with an emphasis on marksmanship, independent action and endurance in unfamiliar places such as the thickly wooded forests of North America.

The light infantry had lighter weapons, carbines, and were less encumbered than the troops of the line, who had to carry entrenching equipment in their field packs as well as miscellaneous squad gear (including cooking pots and the Y-shaped rod designed for stacking arms, but more useful as a spit should a farmer's chicken happen to supplement their rations).

*   *   *

To fight the Americans George III had tried unsuccessfully to buy Russian manpower from Catherine the Great at a low price. After unfavorable intervention by Frederick the Great, however, he had to turn to the more than 300 German princelings, succeeding with those states allied in one way or another to his own family's House of Hanover. These states supplied nearly 30,000 men for the war with the rebellious colonies, some 12,000 not returning to their homelands. A good half, or perhaps more, cited as missing in action, were deserters who forged a new life for themselves in the young republic.

The principality of Hesse-Cassel, in west-central Germany, supplied both the best and the greatest number of these troops—more than half—and gave their name to military history: Hessians.* As it was, one-quarter of the available males in that principality saw service in America.

The German green-coated Jaeger, or hunter, units are not to be confused with the British light infantry. True, their duties included flanking and skirmishing as well as using their marksmen as snipers against a fortified position, but they were not, as was the light infantry, the commandoes of their day. One could say they were semi-irregular fighters, not intended for backwoods Indian fighting as was the light infantry, but still very flexible. They were trained to fight in areas with terrain too difficult for regulars to do their fighting in line, and to take

---

*In addition to Hesse-Cassel and Brunswick (Braunschweig, near Hannover), four other states contributed their manpower: Anhalt-Zerbst, Anspach-Bayreuth, Hesse-Hanau, and Waldeck.

advantage of sudden opportunities. When General Sullivan's command disintegrated in the Battle of Brooklyn, it was the Jaegers who exploited his retreat.

As for the ordinary enlisted man, about the only difference between the British soldier and the German mercenary—usually both from agrarian communities—was that the poor German did not have the brief pleasure of getting drunk while being enlisted.

Stephen Popp, a German soldier, wrote in his diary:

> It was reported to all companies and made known in the Regiment that we must take the road within three weeks. Col. von Voit would assume command. At the same time, young lads from all walks of life were brought in as recruits. Then there occurred a lamentation. Fathers, mothers, and relatives came daily and visited their sons, brothers and friends. . . . Some from sorrow and dislike could hardly be consoled over the fact that they should be torn away from their parents. Wherever you looked you heard nothing but moaning and groaning.[3]

Despite the way they were recruited (read: dragooned), the Germans were good fighters. The French, with an almost two-to-one advantage in manpower, were fought to a standstill in the Seven Years' War by a coalition of small German states—Brunswick, Hesse, and Hannover—supported by token English and Prussian formations.

The German troops were, literally, sold by their rulers, rounded up by raiding parties and disciplined enough to fight well for anyone appointed to lead them. The Duke of Brunswick, for instance, gathered 4,300 men for service in America for the price in pounds sterling of 11,517/17/1 and 1/2 penny, or about $200,000 at today's going rate of exchange, for the first year and twice that for each of the following two years. In addition, he collected "head money" of more than £7 sterling for each man furnished. And finally, there was a damaged-goods proviso in the contract, giving Brunswick an additional £7 for each man killed, three wounded men counting for one dead.

*   *   *

Except for some mounted infantry and some German Jaeger regiments, both the British and German troops were supplied with the muzzle-loading, smooth-bore "Brown Bess" musket. It fired a .75 caliber, or ¾-inch diameter, lead ball. Fitted with a bayonet, it weighed, in all, eleven pounds. The weapon was probably named after the Brown Bill, a halberd or bill axe painted a dull brown which was a common weapon for foot soldiers until the 18th century. Introduced by John Churchill, Duke of Marlborough around 1690, the Brown Bess continued to be the standard British infantry weapon, being used by some units up to the Crimean War in 1854.

Although it had a built-in lateral error of three feet in 100 yards, such a weapon could be devastating when fired by volleys in the close-order fighting common to the day. Its maximum effective range, when used by a mass of troops, was from 80 to 100 yards (about a block and a half in today's Brooklyn).* Often, for the first shot in any anticipated smooth-bore volley firing, the soldiers would add a palmful of tacks or bits of scrap metal to the charge. This decreased the overall effective killing range, but the added metal greatly increased the chance of casualties. Wounded men, after all, are a greater burden to opposing forces than dead soldiers.

For volley firing, the soldiers would face the enemy in a number of ranks (usually three in Western European armies, to six or perhaps eight in the Russian Army), packed shoulder to shoulder. The standard at the time for the infantry was 21 inches for each man in the line. One rank stood to discharge its weapons, the others reloading behind the firing line, or ready to fire, kneeling in the front to be out of the way. This kneeling ready line took care to be behind the muzzles of those firing. When the one discharged its pieces, the next ready would rise, uncover the firing pan, which held the priming gunpowder, cock the flintlock — the action of which would ignite the primer — and fire on command, as the other ranks reloaded.

As the American Revolution progressed, the number of ranks in a line decreased to two, the line widening correspondingly. This new system maintained the same intensity of volley fire while reducing the

---

*British Major George Hanger noted: "A soldier must be very unfortunate indeed who shall be wounded by a musket at 150 yards. . . and as to firing at a man at 200 yards. . . you may just as well fire at the moon and have the same hopes of hitting your object."

number of soldiers who would be targets.

In this hard line of fighting, speed was of the essence. Paper cartridges to hold the ball and powder were made up in advance — there was no time for measuring the charge from the frontiersman's powder horn — and soldiers were trained to "load and fire fifteen times in three minutes and three quarters."[4] But this was on the drill field under perfect conditions. In reality, there were seldom more than two or three volleys in the average encounter.* If called upon, the experienced soldier who could keep his mind on the job could get off a little more than two rounds a minute.

To use the paper cartridge, the soldier bit off the end of the paper cylinder holding the ball and powder,† poured some of the powder into the firing pan, closed the pan's cover and poured the rest of it down the barrel. He then stuffed the paper in the muzzle to act as a vapor barrier to trap the burning gases, dropped the lead ball in, and forced the wad of paper and ball down the barrel with a ramrod. If the earth was hard, the soldier could rest the butt of the weapon on it and seat the ball more quickly. If the ground was wet and soft, as it was during the Battle of Brooklyn, then it took a little more time. In continued firing, powder residue clogged the barrel, making the ramming and seating of the ball more difficult. The flint ignited the powder in the pan through heat caused by the friction, not by the sparks. It struck a "fizzen," as it was called — a dish-shaped steel receptacle — creating a heat of about 400 degrees Fahrenheit, which ignited the priming powder that, in turn, through the touch hole, ignited the main charge. Flints lasted for no more than about fifty uses. Often, the flint would strike and nothing

---

*This approximation, two to three rounds, seems to have been the accepted figure at the time. At The Cowpens, on January 17, 1781, General Daniel Morgan, who had a very low opinion of the qualities of the militia, told these men they could leave after firing two shots in the battle to come. The ensuing concentration of fire — given with great speed — followed by the rapid disappearance of the militia threw the British into confusion, which Morgan, with his regular infanty and cavalry, took advantage of to win the battle.

†Recruits for the American Army at the time were required to have at least four good teeth, two upper and two lower, which had to meet to allow them to bite off the end of the cartridge.

would happen — or the primer would go off and the gun not, whence the phrase "flash in the pan."

In all the confusion and noise of the battle, the soldier might not be able to tell whether his gun had actually discharged its ball. There have been many cases cited of men, repeatedly firing only in the pan and ramming down the barrel more charges. When eventually, the original charge took fire, the expanding gases would be trapped by the extra charges, usually ripping the barrel at its breech, the gun exploding in the soldier's hands.

If a soldier noticed that his musket had not discharged its ball, he could add more powder to the firing pan, cock the striker and try again. If a few such attempts failed, his best choice would be to rely on his bayonet for the remainder of the engagement. To retrieve the ball was too time-consuming in the heat of battle; the soldier would have to use a corkscrew-like device on the end of his ramrod, needing to drive its steel screw into the softer lead of the ball. When he succeeded in securing the ball, it might take much more force to pull it out than it took to insert it. After this operation, the firing mechanism required a good cleaning, particularly a clearing out of the touch hole.

Wet weather added to the difficulties. Should a gunstock swell in heavy rain, it would either misalign or jam the spring that drove the flint against its striker.

Keeping one's head and maintaining volley fire while standing in the ranks had its difficulties, but they were nothing compared to maintaining volley fire during a charge. The charge, at this time — except among Scottish units* — was seldom the wild running toward the enemy of earlier and later wars, but a deliberate march in formation to the cadence of the drumbeat, with bayonets fixed. Soldiers fired from the hip, spraying the foe. To continue to throw volley after volley into the enemy as you approached him was a desirable skill and one both the British and German forces had been trained to accomplish. Training in

---

*The Scots preferred the mad, overwhelming rush at the enemy, trusting that their speed, size and bloodcurdling yells would have an unnerving effect. Often, they would participate in combined cavalry–infantry actions, clinging to the saddles to add additional speed to their own bayonet charge, especially when going uphill.

field evolutions and volley firing was intense in European armies, the goal being to make each regiment an automatic shooting machine.

At the same time in the charge, the line had to be maintained. A soldier a few feet ahead of the line would have his eardrums ruptured by the next volley. The charge, before it quickened during the American Revolution, was a slow affair, marching at one step per second and with many halts to dress the line. In actual battle, the success of the line-dressed charge depended on almost perfect drill-field conditions. The ground had to be obstacle-free, dry and hard, and preferably flat, or at least when sloping, to be free from undulations so as to allow the unit both to maintain its formation and go through the process of loading that was made more complicated by the presence of a bayonet.

While volley fire was used for its initial shock value, the battle was finished with the bayonet, fixed either by a collar to the muzzle to allow firing, as with the Brown Bess, or simply plugged into the muzzle to turn the musket into a spear. The blade, ranging in length from about 18 inches to two feet, was triangular, its base about one inch wide. The two upper sides had indentations known as "blood grooves" to allow easier extraction. The delta-shaped wounds made with this blade were more feared than the bone-crushing ones made by musket balls. The triangular form of the blade left a piercing wound, one inch on a side, which at best would heal slowly. Such wounds were too gaping to be sutured effectively. Instead, treatment might be the application of some type of moss to the wound, under bandages. Even with the moss, these wounds would often fester and bring slow death, several weeks or months after they were received. On the American side, bayonets were used only by a small number of units, primarily those from Delaware and Maryland, who had standardized weapons.

As with the bayonet, the British had a commanding edge with artillery. While the Americans had had some experience in the limited actions of the French and Indian War, they had almost no practice with artillery in fighting on land, cannon being too unwieldy to drag through the dense forests of the New World. (When Colonel Henry Knox removed some 59 of the 200 cannon at Fort Ticonderoga and Crown Point to aid in the siege of Boston, he waited until winter when the deep snow would allow easier transport of the guns on sledges.)

Most of the field pieces in the war were guns firing shot that ranged from three to 24 pounds. These were short-range, smooth-bore pieces, basically clumsy weapons designed to throw a lot of iron in the general direction of the enemy. The field pieces, despite their large-wheeled carriages, were difficult to transport and deploy. Six-pounders weighed from 600 pounds upward, depending on their construction. The wire guns, with a slim barrel wrapped tightly with wire to strengthen it, were the lightest. Brass cannon fell in the middle, and cast iron were the heaviest, varying greatly in weight depending on the foundry. The "new" model 6-pounder cast during the Revolution weighed about 650 pounds for barrel and trunnions, the two projecting pivots to which the carriage was attached. The larger-bore weapons weighed more in proportion, with 24-pounders and larger, usually confined to the decks of ships of the line or on ramparts in fortifications, or dragged up for siege work.

Six-pounders generally threw an iron cannonball, about halfway in size between a baseball and a softball. Ten-pound shot, popular with the Navy, was about the size of a softball. Shot, if the gunpowder was of good quality, left a cannon's muzzle at about 730 feet per second, or 500 miles an hour, retaining enough momentum, even while rolling on the ground, to take off a man's foot.

During the siege of Boston, the American side was so short of artillery ammunition that a bounty was offered for every British cannon-ball collected. The men in the trenches tried to catch them as they rolled after landing, however, the loss of limbs that followed this sport caused the American command to rescind the bounty.

Military jargon of Revolutionary days was optimistic at best: Artillerymen were not ordered to "move" or "transport" their guns; they were expected to "run" them. But there was little of the dashing horse artillery in the American Revolution, with gunners riding postilion or sitting, holding on for dear life, on the ammunition box, or caisson, as it lurched on its two-wheeled limber between team and gun. Such scenes belong to the Napoleonic wars after the modernization of the French artillery by Louis XVI just before the French Revolution. Teams of men specifically trained and assigned to this new corps gave Napoleon the edge in mobility and firepower until the other nations had rearmed by the turn of the century. The British Royal Horse Artillery was established in 1793.

In the 18th century, cannon were "run" by whatever animal was handy, ranging from elephant to man, with bullocks the most preferred. Artillery drivers at the time were little more than teamsters, on foot with long whips to keep the animals moving. Shot and powder followed in such farm carts as could be requisitioned.

At their best, cannon of the time, and those up until the introduction of the rifled Parrott gun in the U.S. Civil War, could send their projectiles no more than a good 120 yards with the assurance of perhaps hitting the side of a barn 50 percent of the time. The smooth-bore cannon could indeed send a projectile farther—a mile or more with a 9-pounder—with the hope of hitting some place in a small town. In this period, cannon were used primarily to weaken an opposing force before an infantry attack, or in sieges to break down defensive works.

It was not until the Napoleonic Wars, with their almost geometric expansion in firepower, men and casualties, that artillery came into its own. It was this later period that saw the common use of rolling barrages to clear advances, aerodynamic hollow shells for greater range, the use of canister, bar, link, chain and grape shot to annihilate masses of the opposition, and the systematic surgical reduction of fortifications with repeated, relatively concentrated fire on a single point.

State-of-the-art, if not advanced, in its equipment, the British Army was the best fighting machine in the world during the latter half of the 18th century. Its officers were haughty and its men proud—and with reason, considering their past successes. They could smash their way through five or more times their number of proper troops. And now, they faced this rabble. . . .

1. The British evacuated Boston on March 17, 1776. Though a temporary strategic setback, a much greater opportunity to quash the rebellion presented itself when the main colonial forces assembled in New York.

2. A New York street scene from *Harper's Weekly,* 1880, depicting life just before the Revolution.

3. A view of the Narrows between Brooklyn and Staten Island with the British fleet assembling.

4. A ground's eye view of the fleet off Staten Island—the largest expeditionary force the British had assembled to that time.

The Americans prepared for the invasion by building fortifications in the New York area. 5. Above, the fort at Horn's Hook. 6. Below, the redoubt at Valley Grove, near Battle Pass in today's Prospect Park.

7. General Sir William Howe was named commander-in-chief of British forces in North America in 1775. Though he failed to destroy Washington's army, he ended his career undefeated in battle.

8. At the time of the Battle of Brooklyn, George Washington lacked Howe's experience in commanding troops, but displayed a formidable intellect and a dynamic talent for improvisation.

9. The Hessians were "rented" to King George III by the rulers of several central German principalities, primarily Hesse-Cassel, near Hannover.

10. At Fort Moultrie, near Charleston, South Carolina, American shore batteries inflicted heavy casualties on elements of the British fleet, news of which heartened the defenders around New York.

11. To test American defenses around New York, the *Phoenix* and the *Rose* sailed up the Hudson River, suffering little damage, though they were attacked by both shore batteries and fire ships.

12. Denyse's Ferry, now Fort Hamilton, site of the first British landings in Brooklyn.

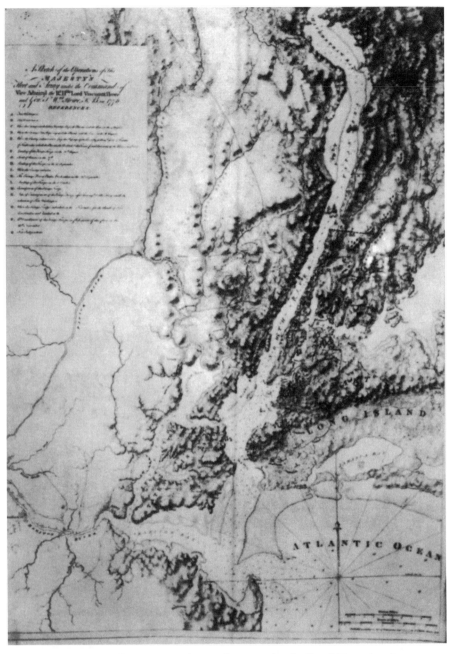

13. A chart of the New York area drawn up by the Royal Navy showing depths, topography and the location of British warships late in 1776.

CHAPTER IV

"A multitude of people...under very little discipline, order or government"

MILITARILY, THE AMERICAN ARMY was in pitiable shape. Had Washington all the units he had been promised, and had they been up to organizational strength, he might have led an army of around 50,000. As it was, the united colonies still had much to learn from the British about undertaking large military operations.

On June 27, 1776, the New York Provincial Congress began recruiting men to fulfill its quota of some 3,000 for the Continental Army. These recruits, the Congress hoped, would be able-bodied, sober and men of good reputation" and it had stressed the word "sober" in its instructions to the county recruiting committees. There was no rush to join the colors by New York City's men, and within a week the Provincial Congress reversed itself, giving recruiting officers a liquor allowance and listing a number of taverns as official stations for securing volunteers.

Still, as a consequence of apathy, unwillingness, or even total ineptitude, or, in the case of the Staten Island Militia and two volunteer regiments from Westchester, going over to the British side at their first opportunity, the contribution in manpower to the American cause by residents of the New York City area was slim.

In an attempt to know how many troops he would actually have to work with, Washington inaugurated what is still an institution in today's army, the Morning Report, called at the time "Returns." Each morning, when American soldiers fell in for muster, the lowest non-commissioned officer would note the number of able troops, those sick or wounded and those missing, whence comes the response to the next highest echelon of command, "All, present or accounted for."

Nevertheless, by the time of the Battle of Brooklyn, Washington had collected, some say, 29,000 troops on paper, the majority of them from New England and the earlier battles around Boston. Most of the rest came from upstate New York, New Jersey, Pennsylvania, Delaware and Maryland.

Although the Americans shared a military tradition with the British, and although their unit structure — at least at the beginning of the war — was similar, the Revolutionary army was less homogeneous than its opponent. In the Battle of Brooklyn, Washington's army would be composed of units from eight states under 13 distinct governmental jurisdictions. Each unit reflected the characteristics of its origins: different terms of service, regulations, training and equipment. Effectiveness, morale and discipline varied from regiment to regiment. At best, Washington's army was a collection of inexperienced volunteers and conscripts — armed with everything from Kentucky rifles to blunderbusses, should the trooper be lucky enough to even own a firearm.

Some Continental Army soldiers and members of the various provincial militias had to make do with stands of pikes — long wooden poles with pointed steel tips. The problem of soldiers without individual firearms was solved in part by Colonel Henry Knox, who needed to find ten-man crews for his 121 cannon in place throughout the New York theater before the battle. To fill his ranks, he borrowed four men from each Continental Army company — their arms, if they had them, to be used by others in the unit — thus gaining artillerymen without reducing the relative firing strength of the companies borrowed from.

Although there was no shortage of patriotic firebrands, revolutionary fervor seemed to be lacking in the ranks of many units. What was written of the Massachusetts Continental Line could also apply to units from Virginia and Maryland: "... poor farmers, young and almost totally indifferent to the course of independence, who were enticed into service by the promise of land, steady wages and easy discipline."[1] The Marylanders, who were to earn the accolade of "immortals" at Brooklyn, joined "not because of a sense of duty or patriotism but [because] Maryland society offered them few opportunities for employment."[2]

Compared to all the British general and field-grade officers, and most of their subalterns, who were professional soldiers and veterans of many campaigns in America, Europe and elsewhere, the Americans facing them were truly citizen soldiers. Few had seen much action; fewer still had any history of extended military service. Washington's officers also reflected the democratic nature of the army. Many of the lower grades were elected by their men, and the appointment of generals was often a compromise between military abilities and political sensitivities, often to the detriment of effectiveness in the field.

General Charles Henry Lee, who had helped build the defenses in Brooklyn, was probably the most experienced on the American side, but apart from during a campaign in Portugal under Burgoyne, he had not had extensive field command. He was present in Braddock's expedition to western Pennsylvania against Fort Duquesne in 1755, along with the young George Washington. Lee had also been an aide and advisor to Stanislaus Poniatowski, the King of Poland, in its civil war and named general in the Polish Army in 1769. While he saw action in the war with Turkey (1769–70), his title was less a description of command than honorific. In his dealings with others he was often contentious. The Iroquois called him "boiling water."

George Washington himself had little actual military experience. In 1755 he was an aide to Braddock in Pennsylvania, but saw no action in the campaign. Later that year, at age twenty-three, he was named colonel and commander-in-chief of the Virginia forces, automatically becoming a brigadier in 1758 when the colony expanded its militia to two regiments (a brigade). Washington and the Virginians served with General John Forbes in a short campaign, once more against Fort Duquesne in 1758. In all, his experience was confined to what fighting he had done in the wilderness: a series of disjointed skirmishes with no opportunity to exercise field evolutions and deployment, and no command of cavalry or artillery.

Nonetheless, Washington, in the war to come, had a natural

advantage over the well-practiced British commanders he faced. Despite his relative lack of a military history and his need to learn as the war progressed, he answered the dictum of Clausewitz, who posited that "a remarkable, superior mind and strength of character"[3] are better qualifications in a commander than an extensive military background.

A few of the American commissioned and non-commissioned officers had had experience in the French and Indian War, a small theater action of the global conflict of the Seven Years' War, which devastated Europe and ranged as far east as Pondichéry in India. Some had served at the Battle of Havana during this conflict. Their experience, however, was more of savage guerrilla skirmishing than of the traditional European warfare expected to be fought in Brooklyn. Most of the American troops had attended militia "training days," which were in fact little more than convivial gatherings that might today be called "male bonding" but in earlier times were more like drinking holidays in the small towns and settlements of the new country.

While they formed the larger part of his troops, the militias of the various colonies were problematical for Washington. A few units were very well trained and equipped; the vast majority were not.

Before the Revolution, the colonial militias were organized along British lines as volunteer, county-based home guards composed of neighbors, usually electing their own officers. In fact, their charters, or papers of incorporation, were similar to those of churches or fraternal organizations. They trained perfunctorily a few days a year, and were called out primarily to guarantee the peace and support civil power. Were they to leave their home county, a portion would be required by their charter to remain at home for local protection. Depending on the province and the county, this local protection might include defense against Indian incursions or slave uprisings. In New York, for instance, the militia's charter required one-third of its men to stay behind.*

---

*Slave risings were always a pervasive concern. In 1741, when those who wrote the militia regulations were in their most impressionable years, there was a rising in New York, the "Negro Revolt," which was swiftly crushed, ten slaves being burned at the stake. Included in the regulations of the New York Militia was a proviso that, when leaving a district, a detachment of the militia was to be left "to guard against the insurrection of slaves."[4]

According to the 1775 Militia Law of the New York Colony, most white males from sixteen to fifty years were eligible for service, with those up to sixty liable to be called in case of invasion. Women and slaves certainly were ineligible, as were Quakers and Catholics as well as ministers, physicians, civil servants, firemen and schoolmasters. Later in the Revolution, these rules were relaxed to encourage others, particularly slaves — with the promise of freedom after the war — to join up.

In the case of service outside a home province, as required in the American Revolution, the units were lent with various degrees of generosity to the central government and subject to recall if needed locally. Eventually, the U.S. government established the power of federalizing the state militias and blending them with the regular army under sole command of the President as commander-in-chief, to serve "for the duration." As "democratic warfare" developed, these units of citizen soldiers, which are now called the National Guard, became immediate sources of organized but relatively untrained men to provide sheer numbers for mobilization.

During the war, Washington constantly pressed for a standing army, although the civilian government remained half-hearted at best. Its demurrals were based in part on a fear of the diminution of the rights of the individual colonies (states) and in part on an abhorrence of the potential for a military dictatorship.* As Washington observed, the army given him was "a multitude of people . . . under very little discipline, order or government." He added that the average soldier "regarded an officer as no more than a broomstick."[5]

In an explanation after the Battle of Brooklyn, on August 30th, of why he had fallen back to Manhattan, Washington wrote to the New York Convention: "It is the most intricate thing in the world, Sir, to know how to conduct one's self in respect to the Militia; if you do not

---

*The Second Amendment of the U.S. Constitution addressed both these fears. It allows the states to keep military forces, guaranteeing "the right of the people to keep and bear arms." This principle was deemed sufficient to ensure that the states' militias would be strong enough to deter any coup by a Federal army. During shrinkages of the regular army, in 1783, 1865 and 1919, the states in combination could in fact field a force larger than the army of the United States. This principle was also applied with the mobilization of the Confederate States' militias in 1861.

begin many days before they are wanted to raise them, you cannot have them in time; if you do, they get tired and return, besides being under very little order or government while in service."[6]

Some units, however, were fully trained and equipped. Washington used these as a cadre, or backbone, to strengthen the masses of untrained and undisciplined other troops. Commenting on these "well formed regiments," which figured prominently in the bloodiest action in the Battle of Brooklyn, Washington would cite his need of them, declaring that "our liberties" could be lost "if their defense is left to any but a permanent standing army." He had watched the local militias "almost by whole regiments" disappear, the field to be held only by the toughness, loyalty and valor of such units as Haslet's Delawares or Smallwood's Maryland Regiment.[7] After the battle, an English officer remembered the Delaware unit, ". . . their ranks full, their uniforms smart. . . their courage high."[8]

Although only one-quarter, 1,000, of the number the Maryland Council of Safety had promised Congress on August 16th, Smallwood's regiment was commanded by the chivalry of the colony's old Catholic families. The Council wrote: "We shall have with you in a few days four thousand men, which is all that we can arm and equip, and the people of New York, for whom we have great affection, can have no more than our all."[9] After Brooklyn, the next Maryland contingent arrived in time to reinforce Smallwood's depleted unit and fight in the Battle of White Plains, October 28th. Unlike the average militia unit, Maryland's soldiers were fully equipped and very well drilled. In Maryland, Smallwood's regiment was known as "The Dandy Fifth"; when it arrived in New York, its men were called "macaronis" by the rest of the army.

* * *

The Americans, for the most part, brought their guns from home and had every type imaginable. The difference of bore made issuance of standardized ammunition impossible. In Brooklyn, the Kentucky or Pennsylvania long rifle appeared in some numbers, being the preferred weapon of farmers, who chose it for its accuracy, economy and long range for bagging game. Because its users could hit a target the size of a deer's brain at 150 yards, the rifle was the most appropriate weapon for pickets on guard duty in advanced positions, as well as for flankers, skirmishers and snipers. Indeed, a Major Hanger, who had a low opinion of the smooth-bore musket, noted: "I am certain that, provided an American rifleman was to get a perfect aim at 300 yards at me standing still, he most undoubtedly would hit me unless it was a very windy day."[10]

Contrary to popular belief, the long rifle was neither the weapon of choice once the American forces were being re-armed, nor was it the most commonly used firearm in the war.

However accurate, the use of the long rifle was limited in the traditional battle, which depended on the rapid volley fire only the musket could supply. The rifles, with their long barrels, were difficult and slow to load. They used a smaller ball, about one-half inch, or in today's designation, .50 caliber or less, as opposed to the 3/4-inch musket ball (with its much greater stopping power). The smaller ball was large enough to bring down any game the thrifty farmers and frontiersmen found in the American backwoods, and small enough not to be wasteful of lead. But because of the rifling and the need for a tight fit to make the most efficient use of the burning gases, the lead ball had to be pounded home with an iron ramrod and a wood mallet.* In addition to the difficulty of loading, the long rifle's accuracy over a great distance was of little consequence in the heavily forested site of the Battle of Brooklyn.

In the battle to come, most of the Americans had no bayonets, these being used only by a small number of units, primarily the aforementioned from Delaware and Maryland, who had standardized weapons. About the only edged weapon the Americans had, apart from officers' swords or those issued to the cavalry, were tomahawks, which were regulation. The tomahawk, however, was used more as a universal tool (as the GI's in World War II and Korea used their bayonets) than as a weapon of war.

---

*These long rifles averaged 4'10" from end to end. The ramrod was about 33" long, making the total length of the instrument at the time of loading about 7'7". One might suppose Americans were much taller then, or that the rifleman might have brought a stool with him or hoped to find a rock to stand on. In practice, they found a convenient tree trunk or stone to load the weapon diagonally.

Considering how the Americans took to privateering during the earlier intercolonial wars, and in various ventures to circumvent British trade restrictions, they had considerable experience in using cannon *at sea,* which helped provide a cadre of technicians for the American artillery. At least a number of Americans knew how to load, aim and shoot a cannon, if not deploy it in a land battle. The Father of the American Artillery, Colonel, later General, Henry Knox, a Boston bookseller in civilan life, learned his trade from reading military works he stocked for British officers. (Actually books were only a small part of his trade—before joining the American Army, Knox prudently conducted a "going out of business sale," offering, among other items, kitchen furniture, books, prints, assorted paper hangings, mathematical instruments, hunting whips, and fifes for military use.)

*   *   *

Complicating Washington's difficulties was the matter of supplies. The great variety of firearms caused its own special nightmare for supply officers. What food, uniforms and medical supplies were acquired were almost impossible to distribute through a lack of organization—from commissary to medical. And lack of foresight complicated things.

A small example was the matter of supplying uniforms. As long as the soldiers were adequately clothed, putting them in uniform had a low priority. Uniforms were, however, found useful to instill pride, establish organization and enforce discipline—if only because a soldier in a uniform with regimental markings was more easily identified by a civilian with a complaint. Moreover, deserters—the bane of armies, particularly considering the recruiting practices of the 18th century—found it more difficult to blend in with the general population.

In its effort to provide uniforms, a few months earlier in the year the New York Provincial Assembly had made a good buy in linen and started to issue the troops coats and trousers in that fabric. Linen is easily washed and is comfortable in the warmth of a New York summer. But as every housewife of the period knew, and most of the men who made the purchase should have known, linen was no material to wear near fire, or even sparks, such as those produced by the firing of a flintlock, considering the material's high degree of flammability. The British troops might suffer from the August heat in their pressed-wool uniforms, but they were better protected from incineration in the fires of battle.

While the average American soldier at the beginning of the war wore whatever he brought from home, Washington did encourage his men to wear a frontiersman's hunting shirt. This could be more easily supplied than the regimentals worn by the fully equipped Delaware and Maryland units. While the shirt also provided a sense of conformity, Washington saw a psychological value to its wearing and continued to urge its use throughout the war. The British regular, he believed, was in terror of the long-range accuracy of the American rifle. Writing later in the war, Washington noted that the British believed "every such person [who wore the frontier shirt] a complete Marksman."[11]

A Hessian account of the Battle of Brooklyn would comment on the American turnout: "Not a single regiment is regularly uniformed or armed; every one has his private musket, just as the Hessian citizens march out on Whitsuntide [for the annual muster of civilian militia], except Stirling's regiment, which had a blue and red uniform, was three battalions strong, and consisted mostly of Germans enlisted in Pennsylvania. They were tall, fine men, and had very fine English muskets with bayonets."[12]

While the average American soldier was under-equipped and poorly clothed during much, if not all, of the war, the leadership did make honest efforts to equip their fighting men. The men's table of equipment was more carefully thought out and more generous than that in many other armies of the time. Shortages of money and procurement and distribution difficulties, however, plagued supply efforts throughout the war.

At least in theory, the Continental Army soldier was to be issued a regimental coat, waistcoat, garters, one pair of shoes, two pairs of knee britches or overalls (trousers), two white shirts, a neckstock and a cocked hat. For fatigue duty he could receive a fatigue hat, hunting or frock coat — not the formal knee-length coat of the Victorian era, but more of a shift or rough jacket — a pair of hunting pants or overalls, moccasins, a linen or leather apron and a belt.

Personal equipment included: cup, plate, knife, fort and spoon, candle lantern and candles, tinder box with flint, steel for striking sparks and charred linen tinder, a sewing kit, soap, musket-cleaning cloths, a blanket, an oiled cloth to serve as a poncho or ground cloth, and a canteen, haversack and knapsack. In the winter he was to be issued a wool hat, scarf and sweater, extra shoes, extra blankets, gloves or mittens, wool or sheepskin leg wrappings with leather strapping, a cloak, blanket coat or overcoat and ice creepers — metal flanges secured under the arch by a strap for greater traction over frozen ground.

In addition to his musket and bayonet with scabbard, flints, cartridges, cartridge box and sling, pocket or belt knife and belt axe (tomahawk), the patriot soldier was to be issued a plug for the musket barrel and musket tools.

*   *   *

On paper, the Americans fielded a formidable army. In addition to the troops General Washington had brought with him from Boston, 13,000 more of the militia were ordered to join him by the Continental Congress, which also directed the organization of a reserve corps of 10,000. These 23,000, however, never materialized. What's more, half of the militia that Washington had been counting on in Queens and Kings Counties was ordered to join General Greene in Hempstead, Long Island, and stay there until September.

At thirty-four, Nathanael Greene was the youngest flag officer in Washington's command in this theater. His going to Hempstead was a serious problem. He had been in command in Brooklyn for several months and knew the terrain well, but fell ill on August 15th with "camp fever," as typhus was then called. This happened just as the British had completed their massing of troops on Staten Island. Greene's command was transferred to General Sullivan on August 20th. While Washington viewed Sullivan as a capable officer, he lacked complete confidence in him, noting: ". . .[he] has his wants, and he has his foibles. . .a little tincture of vanity and. . .an over-desire of being popular, which now and then leads him into some embarrassments."[13]

Four days before the battle, on the 24th, Sullivan was ordered to relinquish the major part of his command to his senior, General Israel Putnam, who at fifty-eight was the oldest of Washington's generals at

Brooklyn. The lines of command under this new arrangement were not made clear and added to the confusion among subordinate commanders and in the ranks. Putnam was the senior commander and, by and large, in charge. His charismatic outward qualities, his blindness to personal safety, his outstanding valor, his general picturesqueness—he looked the epitome of military effectiveness—endeared him to his men and civilians alike. Stories of his exploits in the French and Indian War and around Boston gave him an almost legendary persona.

But not everyone was enthralled. In the week before the battle, one American wrote that Putnam dashed "along on horseback at fine speed, his uniform consisting of a soiled shirt, over which he wore a sleeveless waistcoat." On these excursions he issued "orders right and left." But these, the soldier noted, seemed to be without "any well defined purpose."[14]

Putnam did perhaps seem better suited for warfare like that against Pontiac's Ottawas, in the battles for Detroit in 1764, than against the cream of the British army in Brooklyn. Prior to the battle Washington had given him very specific orders: "I would have you form proper line of defence around your encampment and works. . . . *The woods should be secured by abatis,* * *etc., where necessary, to make the enemy's approach as difficult as possible.* Traps and ambuscades should be laid for the parties, if you find they are sent out after cattle."[15] Although these orders were delivered early on the 25th, no effort was made to implement them and strengthen the lines.

Putnam's general deficiency in knowledge of tactics was compounded by his absolute ignorance of the ground on which the battle was to be fought. During the battle he never left the inner defenses on Brooklyn Neck. Faithfully following his dictum to fight wherever and whenever he saw an enemy, however, Putnam ordered the Americans under his command not into a unified engagement but into a series of separate and desperate struggles fought almost blindly in the woods and swamps of Brooklyn.

---

*Abatis: a defensive line of felled trees in front of a wall or parapet. These were seldom the neatly trimmed and sharpened line of tree trunks of the movies, but trees laid with branches interwoven to tangle up any opposing infantry trying to cross them.

The battle scenario under Nathanael Greene, on the other hand, was to fight with an elastic defense, holding where he could, but retreating when necessary, and effecting heavy casualties as the American forces had done at Bunker Hill (where the British losses were 50 percent).

Under Putnam, the Americans were set to fight a no-retreat, defensive, static battle, holding on to their fortified positions. Putnam had established no significant "flying camp," as a reserve force was called at the time, or, as the French more appropriately say, *masse de manoeuvre,* to reinforce a threatened position, to take advantage of a weakness in the enemy's advance or, if it became a slugging match, to replace spent troops.

Under Generals Greene and Sullivan, nightly patrols had been kept on the roads across Brooklyn. This vigilance was to be neglected by Putnam and the problem was compounded by his remaining in headquarters behind the lines on Brooklyn Neck, neither touring the site of the anticipated battle nor examining the fortifications or the lines of approach.

As the day of the battle approached, Washington's official roll cited 20,537 troops at its highest point. But of these, nearly 4,000 were on leave or sick. He had received 3,150 more men in July, but these were at best raw recruits—inexperienced, undisciplined and under-equipped. By mid-August, the roll noted 17,225 in all, with 3,668 of these unavailable for action. The effectives, 13,557, were scattered from King's Bridge on the Harlem Creek to the Narrows. The largest concentration may have reached 5,500 men standing along the lines in Brooklyn, with another thousand or two dribbling in during the days immediately preceding the battle, until more were rushed over on the 27th and 28th.

CHAPTER V

"I thought all London was afloat"

WHILE WASHINGTON WAS trying to raise, train and arm his troops, the British were writing the book on mass mobilization, anticipating the maxim attributed to Confederate General Nathan Bedford Forrest of getting there "furstest with the mostest" by eighty-plus years.

General Howe had sailed from Halifax, arriving off Sandy Hook on June 25th with 130 ships and more than 9,000 troops. His brother, the Admiral, arrived on July 12th with about 13,000 soldiers in a fleet of 150 ships. (The combined British fleets were more than double the size of the Spanish Armada, which, though legendary, consisted of only 129 vessels, albeit big ones.)

To gain anchorage off Staten Island, each ship proceeded in line through a channel in the harbor's bar of silt, following the lead ship at a distance and correcting its own course with sightings on the Sandy Hook lighthouse and the spire, in Brooklyn, of the New Utrecht Dutch Reformed Church.* Each vessel further corrected its heading when the fort at the Battery on Manhattan Island came in sight.

Ambrose Serle, Admiral Howe's civilian secretary, wrote of the arrival:

---

*The church now standing on the site of the original 1699 building at 18th Avenue and 83rd Street was built from its predecessor's stones in 1828.

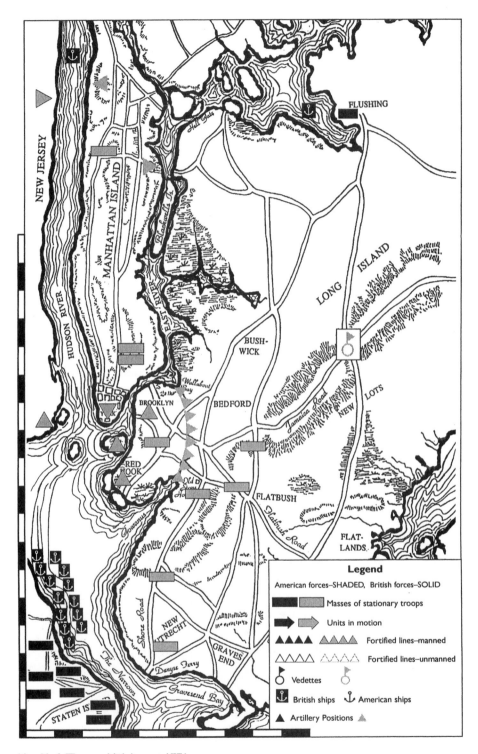

New York Theater, Mid-August 1776

This morning, the sun shining bright, we had a beautiful prospect of the coast of New Jersey at about five or six miles distance. The land was cleared in many places, and the woods were interspersed with houses, which being covered with white shingles appeared very plainly all along the shore. We passed Sandy Hook in the afternoon, and about six o'clock arrived safe off the east side of Staten Island. The country on both sides was highly picturesque and agreeable. Nothing could exceed the joy that appeared throughout the fleet and army upon our arrival. We were saluted by all the ships of war in the harbor, by the cheers of the sailors all along the ships and by those of the soldiers on the shore. . . What added to their pleasure was that this very day about noon the *Phoenix* of forty guns and the *Rose* of twenty, with three tenders, forced their passage up the river in defiance of all [the Americans'] vaunted batteries, and got safe above the town, which will much intercept the provisions of the rebels.[1]

The sight of elements of the fleet sailing untroubled past the strengthened batteries on Governors Island, in Lower Manhattan, and at Paulus Hook brought everyone, citizens and soldiers alike, to the shore to watch. The exchange of gunfire frightened the women and a number of men watching. Said Serle: "When the men-of-war passed up the river, the shrieks and cries of those poor creatures, running every way with their children, was truly distressing and I fear will have an unhappy effect on the ears and minds of our young and inexperienced soldiers."[2]

Civilians as idle spectators were one thing, but Washington took a stern view of American soldiers' lack of attention to their posts: "The General was sorry to observe. . .many of the officers and a number of men instead of attending to their duty at the beat of the drum continued along the banks of the North River, gazing at the ships. Such unsoldierly conduct must grieve every good officer, and give the enemy a *mean* opinion of the army as nothing shows the brave and good soldier more than in case of alarms, coolly and calmly repairing to his post and then waiting his orders, whereas a weak curiosity at such a time makes men look mean and contemptible."[3]

On landing on Staten Island, Admiral Howe tried, on two occasions, to have a letter delivered to Washington to suggest a meeting.

Both attempts failed, probably because Washington doubted that a parlay would be of any use, but at the time the problem seemed to be rooted in protocol. Henry Knox wrote to his wife, Lucy, on July 15th:

[Lord Howe] sent a flag of truce up to the city. They came within about four miles of the city, and were met by some of Colonel Tupper's people, who detained them until his Excellency's pleasure should be known. Accordingly, Colonel Reed [Washington's adjutant general] and myself went down to the barge to receive the message. When we came to them, the officer, who was, I believe, captain of the *Eagle,* man-of-war, rose up and bowed, keeping [on] his hat.

"I have a letter, sir, from Lord Howe to Mr. Washington."

"Sir," says Colonel Reed, "we have no person in our army with that address."

"Sir," says the officer, "will you look at the address?" He took out of his pocket a letter which was thus addressed:

> George Washington, Esq.
> New York
>   Howe

"No sir," says Colonel Reed, "I cannot receive that letter."

"I am very sorry," says the officer, "and so will be Lord Howe, that any error in the superscription should prevent the letter being received by General Washington."

"Why sir," says Colonel Reed, "I must obey orders."

"Oh, yes, sir, you must obey orders, to be sure."

Then, after giving him a letter from Colonel Campbell to General Howe, and some letters from prisoners to their friends, we stood off, having saluted and bowed to each other. After we had got a little way, the officer put about his barge and stood for us and asked by what particular he chose to be addressed.

Colonel Reed said, "You are sensible, sir, of the rank of General Washington in our army?"

"Yes, sir, we are. I am sure my Lord Howe will lament exceedingly this affair, as the letter is quite of a civil nature, and not a military one. He laments exceedingly that he was not here a little sooner."

Which we suppose to allude to the Declaration of Independence, upon which we bowed and parted in the most genteel terms imiginable (*sic*).[4]

A few days later, Knox wrote Lucy that Howe's adjutant general, Colonel Paterson, had met with Washington on July 20th under a flag of truce:

> The purport of his message was in very elegant, polite strains, to endeavor to persuade General Washington to receive a letter directed to George Washington, Esq., etc. etc. In the course of his talk every other word was, "May it please your Excellency," "If your Excellency so please." In short, no person could pay more respect than the adjutant general . . .
>
> He said Lord and General Howe lamented exceedingly that any errors in the direction should interrupt that frequent intercourse between the armies which might be necessary in the course of the service, [and] that Lord Howe had come out with great powers.
>
> [Washington] said he had heard that Lord Howe had come out with very great powers to pardon, but he had come to the wrong place; the Americans had not offended, therefore they needed no pardon.
>
> This confused [Howe's adjutant]. After a considerable deal of talk about the good disposition of Lord and General Howe, he asked, "Has your Excellency no particular commands with which you would please to honor me to Lord and General Howe?"
>
> "Nothing, sir, but my particular compliments to both." — a good answer.[5]

Howe's secretary, Ambrose Serle, was put off by this inability to communicate: "We strove as far as decency and honor could permit . . . to avert all bloodshed. . . . And yet it seems to be beneath a little paltry colonel of banditti rebels to treat with a representative of his lawful sovereign because it is impossible to give all the titles which the poor creature requires."[6]

It was not until the Battle of Yorktown, which essentially ended the war, that the British officially recognized *General* Washington's title.

While the British were attempting to deliver the letter, Admiral Sir Peter Parker joined them on August 1st with the near 3,000-man force of Generals Clinton and Cornwallis, in some 40 ships, returning after an unsuccessful attempt to take Charleston, South Carolina.

On June 28th, the squadron had attacked the garrison on Sullivan's Island, Charleston, and was repulsed by Colonel William Moultrie and 400 men under his command. On seeing this addition to Howe's forces, one British soldier commented: "The arrival of a crippled ship and a defeated officer, at that time, was very unwelcome; for it infused fresh spirits into the rebels, and showed them that ships were sometimes obliged to retreat from batteries."[7] Obviously the Americans who received news of the battle at Charleston would have felt comfort in seeing the defeated troops and damaged ships. However, at the Battle of Fort Moultrie, as it is known, land forces were not engaged and the navy took the majority of the 200-plus casualties. The arrival of the 3,000 British soldiers, whose unit integrity had not been broken, and the sailors in the flotilla, seeking revenge for their bruised honor, was not necessarily good news. Washington found the addition to Howe's forces "alarming."[8]

Admiral Parker also brought with him a few of the Royal Governors displaced from their provinces in the South, as well as some Loyalist Virginia militia, which included a number of black troops.

A force of 8,000 mercenaries from the German principality of Hesse-Cassel completed the army in August. The 14-week crossing was an ordeal for the Hessians, whose homeland was a landlocked province in central Germany. Even the Hessian commander, General de Heister, traveling in relative comfort, had found it a trial. Enlisted men slept six to a bunk designed for four. Drinking water was in such a condition as to require straining, and the main staple, hardtack, required a cannonball to pound it soft. The officers of one unit were relieved, on arrival in Staten Island, that "only 22 men died during the voyage."[9] (Total losses during the passage of the fleets came to about eight percent of Howe's command, or ten times his losses in the battle.)

In all, with the British regulars, Hessians, and a few black regiments from the West Indies — recruited from the slave population with promises of freedom — Howe had about 32,000 trained, disciplined and fully equipped men, not counting the approximately 10,000 sailors (with their contingent of over 2,000 Royal Marines who were to fight on shore in some numbers), 30 warships and 400 transports in the bay. He was in command of the largest and best-equipped expeditionary force the British had ever mounted,* carried on board the largest armada North America had ever seen. And with five months' provisions in the ships' holds, they were here to stay.

One colonist called this flotilla, anchored in the outer bay, a "forest of masts."[10] When the British landed on Staten Island from the assembly point off Sandy Hook at the beginning of July, Daniel McCurtin, a private in the Maryland Brigade, wrote: "I spied as I peeped out the Bay something resembling a wood of pine trees trimmed. . . .In about ten minutes the whole Bay was full of shipping as ever it could be. . . .I thought all London was afloat."[11]

The passage through the Narrows did not go unopposed. A battery of Continental 9-pounders placed on the heights where Fort Hamilton now stands fired on the British ships. The only effect of this bombardment was to carry away the rigging of one tender, kill a sailor and wound nine more. The British 64-gun ship of the line *Asia,* at the end of the column, returned fire with a broadside of her 24-pounders. While impressive, *Asia*'s fire missed the colonial battery. One of her rounds lodged in the wall of the home of a Mr. Bennet, and Denyse Denyse got three, one hitting his barn, another his house, and a third blowing away the garden fence near his front door.

Before the movement through the Narrows, Howe had sent a scouting party ashore at Gravesend Bay to examine the possibility of a direct landing of his forces on Long Island. This party was repulsed by 500 men under the command of General Joseph Spencer. The landing of the British on Staten Island, however, was much more welcome. In a report to London, Howe described the Staten Islanders as "a most loyal

---

*The British did have some experience in mounting overseas expeditions. In 1758 they had sent a force of 11,000 soldiers on about 200 ships manned by 14,000 sailors to lay the second siege of Louisbourg, on Cape Breton Island, Nova Scotia. At least eight of the regiments or brigades at that siege were also in Brooklyn 18 years later. It can be assumed some of the younger enlisted men and officers at Louisbourg were seasoned professionals at Brooklyn.

people, long-suffering on that account under the opposition of the Rebels stationed among them."[12]

The British had dispersed their forces across Staten Island without any resistance on the part of the county militia and with only sporadic objections from the civilians. The militia, for their part, had been in hiding since the first few hours of the landing, before returning to their homes. These local defenders had been recruited with reluctance from a population that had been averse to the progress of the Revolution and indifferent to the actions of the New York Provincial Congress.

Urged to gather and listen to an appeal from Royal Governor Tryon, some four hundred — nearly all of the Staten Island Militia — decided to change sides, swearing, on July 6th, allegiance to the Crown. Although they would not become part of the regular British Army, they were pleased to learn they would receive the regular army pay plus a guarantee that they would be required to serve only as a home guard on the island.

The British then received another addition to their strike force: the New York Volunteers. This unit was formed of Loyalists recruited in Westchester by Joshua Bangs earlier in the year. They provided their own arms and equipment. In such uniforms as they had, they mingled inconspicuously with Washington's troops — entering Manhattan and making it to Staten Island. In the Battle of Brooklyn they served with the British Seventh Brigade.

*   *   *

Staten Island, indeed, was a place of high sympathy for the British. The citizens had declined earlier to vote for the Provincial Congress and remained particularly quiescent during the British occupation to come. Relations between the investing forces and the civilians were for the most part friendly, the expected normal frictions from billeting, appropriating supplies and fraternizing being diminished.

Fraternization, a modern word to describe official displeasure with too much contact between occupiers and the occupied, was not an issue to the common soldier of the 18th century. It seems, as well, a concept unknown to many of the innocent residents. A captain in the Royal Engineers, Francis Rawdon, Lord Hastings, wrote in a letter to his uncle:

The fair nymphs of this isle are in wonderful tribulation, as the fresh meat our men have got here have made them as rioutous (*sic*) as satyrs. A girl cannot step into the bushes to pluck a rose without running the most imminent risk of being ravished, and they are so little accustomed to these vigorous methods that they don't bear them with the proper resignation, and of consequence we have the most entertaining courts-martial every day...

A girl of this island made a complaint the other day to Lord Percy of her being deflowered, as she said, by some grenadiers. Lord Percy asked her how she knew them to be grenadiers, as it happened in the dark. "Oh, good God," cried she, "they could be nothing else, and if your Lordship will examine I am sure you will find it so."[13]

In point of fact, both officers and men were beginning to seek more action than Staten Island offered. Rawdon added: "All the English troops are encamped, or in cantonment upon this island, as healthy and spirited a body of men as ever took the field. . . .[But] some of the Hessians are arrived and long much to have a brush with the rebels, of whom they have a most despicable opinion. They are good troops, but in point of men nothing equal to ours. Some of the Guards are arrived, but not yet landed. Everybody seems to have formed a most favorable opinion of them. . . . I imagine that we shall very soon come to action, and I do not doubt but the consequence will be fatal to the rebels. An army composed as theirs is cannot bear the frown of adversity."[14]

This restlessness was also beginning to show on the American side. As Washington gathered his forces in New York, the delights of the metropolis provided temptations to the, for the most part, country-bred Continentals and militia. As Colonel Loammi Baldwin wrote to his wife:

The whores (by information) continue their employ, which is become very very lucrative. Their unparalleled conduct is sufficient antidote against any desires that a person can have that has one spark of modesty or virtue left in him and the last atum (*sic*) must certainly be lost before he can associate himself with those bitchfoxy jades, jills, hags, strums, prostitutes and these multiplied into one another and then their full character not displayed. Perhaps you will call me censorious and exclaim too much upon bare reports when I say that I was never within the doors of, nor exchanged a day in going to grand round with my guard of escort, having broke up the knots of men and women fighting, pulling caps, swearing, crying, "Murder!" etc., hurried them off to the Provost Dungeon by half dozens, there let them lay mixed till next day. Then some are punished and some get off clear—Hell's work. . . . [15]

Hoping to shape up the troops and also prevent any temptation, Washington issued the following orders:

The gin shops and other houses where liquors have been heretofore retailed within or near the lines. . . are strictly forbidden to sell any for the future to soldiers in the army and the inhabitants of said houses near the lines are immediately to move out of them; they are to be appropriated to the use of the troops.

If any soldier of the army shall be found disgusted with liquor, as has been too much the practice heretofore, the General is determined to have him punished with the utmost severity, as no soldier in such situation can be either fit for defense or attack. The General orders that no sutlers in the army shall sell to any soldier more than one half pint of spirit per day. [16]

One imagines half a pint—eight one-ounce shots—of spirits that averaged around 100 proof is a bit much, but people drank more then. Even though the generations pass, soldiers do not change and the military is slow to learn. In Washington's time, the order on grog shops was stern and the regulations on sutlers (camp followers who functioned as peddlers) precise. But if an extra gill was wanted, a soldier could find it after just a short stagger.

In the wilds of Brooklyn, where life was ever more simple and gentle than in the big city across the river, there were fewer temptations from the women or the grog shops, but Nathanael Greene found reason to improve the decorum of the troops under his command. In a general order, he said: "Complaints have been made by the inhabitants situated near the Mill Pond [on the Gowanus] that some of the soldiers come there to go swimming in the open view of the women and that they come out of the water and run to the houses naked with a design to insult and wound the modesty of female decency, [so] 'tis with concern that the general finds himself under the disagreeable necessity of expressing his disapprobation of such beastly conduct. Whoever has been so void of shame as to act such an infamous part, let them veil their past disgrace by their future good behavior, for they may depend upon it, any new instances of such scandalous conduct will be punished with the utmost severity."[17]

CHAPTER VI

"As we can now bring all our guns to bear..."

D URING THEIR LONG CONTROL of New York, the British had left, for the most part, the defense of the city to their navy. On land there was essentially just one fort, at the southern tip of Manhattan Island, called the Battery, which was part of the official compound that included the governor's residence and an arsenal. Parliament had also voted taxes to build a fort on what would later be called Governors Island in the Upper Bay; however these monies had been misapplied, the governor, Lord Cornbury (1666–1724), electing to build a summer home on the island instead.

Now, with American control of New York, "defense" primarily meant defense against British invasion, both to protect the port city and to prevent their ships from gaining control of the Hudson and dividing the colonies. Writing to Washington, General Charles Lee worried: "What to do with this city, I own it puzzles me. It is so encircled with deep navigable water, that whoever commands the sea must command the town."[1]

Artillery on Brooklyn Heights, however, would command the East River and New York City. If the British held that position, it would be a reversal of the situation the year before, when the Americans held Dorchester Heights overlooking Boston and forced the British to evacuate. To fortify the harbor, therefore, Washington had the old Battery strengthened and gun emplacements sited on Paulus Hook (at

Exchange Place in what is today Jersey City), on Governors Island and on the heights of Brooklyn above the East River. With these batteries, it was hoped, sufficient interlacing firepower would offset what was viewed as a natural advantage of naval weaponry over land-based cannon. Additional guns were to be placed farther south, on Red Hook.

To protect the batteries in Brooklyn, a line of earthworks, later upgraded to forts, was built on the landward side. In July, Washington had formed a special corps to defend the interior fortifications in Brooklyn. In his orders to the corps, he wrote: "The General expects that all soldiers who are entrusted with the defense of any work will behave with great coolness and bravery and will be particularly careful not to throw away their fire; he recommends them to load for their first fire with one musket-ball and four or eight buckshot, according to the size and strength of their pieces. If the enemy is received with such a fire, at not more than twenty or thirty yards distance, he has no doubt of their being repulsed."[2]

Passage up the Hudson was further restricted by forts built approximately where the landings of the George Washington Bridge are now: Fort Constitution (later named Fort Lee) in New Jersey and Fort Washington on Manhattan Island. A log boom was floated between them. Another fort, Independence, was established on the heights of Riverdale, which commanded the Hudson River and the ford on Harlem Creek between Manhattan and today's Bronx. Additional barrier forts and strongpoints were built along the Hudson. A final and hoped-for ultimate barrier to the British fleet was also being worked on: a heavy iron chain across the channel, 40 miles upstream, under the guns of Fort Montgomery at West Point.

To control the northern entry to the East River, a battery was set up at Hoorn's Hook, where Gracie Mansion now stands, about eight miles north of the then-city, within easy cannon range of the tidal races at Hellgate.

The work of building the fortifications in Brooklyn was initially directed by General Lee, who crossed over from Manhattan with a detachment of troops to begin digging on February 18th. The major part of the work, however, was executed by levies of civilians and slaves. In mid-March, Kings County officials were directed by the Provincial

Congress to supply half of their white males and all of their male slaves to work on the fortifications, using their own digging tools. The project was open-ended — the men were to remain on the job until the defenses had been properly erected.

Faced with the inevitable British invasion, Washington's best tactical choice might have been to abandon New York and fall back to Westchester. North of the Harlem Creek his lines of communication would have been shorter, the terrain better known to many more of his commanders than was Brooklyn's, and more favorable to the type of skirmish at which his army was adept. This position would also have offered fewer opportunities for the British to use their fleet to advantage.

Indeed, as the pressure mounted in the late spring and early summer of 1776, John Jay proposed in the Continental Congress that New York City be burned, Long Island be laid waste, and the army and city inhabitants fall back to the Hudson Highlands in the Ramapo Mountains from Suffern to West Point.*

Washington chose to hold on to the city, however, and he placed the bulk of his army in what could be a trap even for an experienced, fully equipped and organized armed force — three qualities his army, made up of militia and short-term soldiers, did not possess.

He split his army between Manhattan and Long Island, with the East River between them. Columbia Heights, now Brooklyn Heights, dominating both the river and the City of New York, was vital as an artillery position. A strongly fortified battery on the 100-foot elevation as well as gun emplacements on Governors Island, and one facing them at the Battery in Manhattan, might deter, or at least slow, a movement by Black Dick's ships of the line up the channel. Governors Island was

---

*Even with today's mechanized fighting forces, the Hudson Highlands present a formidable defensive position. The triangular area, ten miles on a side, is a plateau with the average initial climb through dense underbrush rising 400 feet for each 350 feet on the horizontal — a more than a 45-degree slope. The terrain was so difficult of access that it became a refuge for criminals and runaway slaves. One pirate, Claudius Smith, who ranged as far as Long Island Sound, successfully fought off repeated attempts by regular army units to storm his den, only a third of a mile on the map, but 600 feet above the village of Tuxedo, NY. In the time of the Revolution, this area's natural assets — high-quality iron ore and a vast hardwood forest — were used extensively to supply armaments to the American forces.

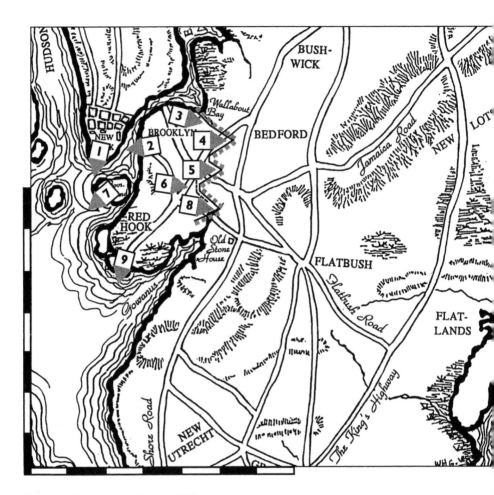

American Dispositions, August 1776

Forts:

1. The Battery	6. Cobble Hill	Trench Lines ▪▪▪▪▪▪▪▪
2. Fort Stirling	7. Governors Island	
3. Fort Putnam	8. Fort Box	Palisade added August 27th
4. Ring Fort	9. Fort Defiance	
5. Fort Greene		▬ ▬ ▬ ▬ ▬ ▬ ▬ ▬

particularly well fortified. General Israel Putnam and 1,000 men crossed to the island on April 9th and worked overnight building breastworks. On April 16th, the Bunker Hill Regiment (7th Colonial Infantry) under Colonel Prescott and the 4th Colonial Infantry, under Colonel Nixon, occupied the island, extending earthworks and sinking hulks in the main channel. The hulks were connected by a chevaux-de-frieze, a log boom with tree trunks attached, to ensnare a ship's rudder and, hopefully, make it a sitting target for the four 32-pound cannon and four 18-pounders on the island.

This battery was backed up by the one on Red Hook, which, a Major Shaw noted, was "situated in such a manner as to command the harbor entirely. . . . We have a fort with four 18-pounders, to fire *en barbette,* that is, over the top of the works, which is vastly better than firing through embrasures, as we can now bring all our guns to bear on the same object at once. The fort is named Defiance."[3]

Despite Major Shaw's optimism, the British ships of the line mounted 24- and 32-pound guns as a matter of course, and some, such as the *Asia,* had heavier firepower: each ship could fire broadsides of 12 to 30 cannon. Should the British fleet move north into the East River it would separate the contingents in Brooklyn and Manhattan and subject both sides of the river to heavy shelling. *Asia,* for instance, had a throw weight from one broadside of 1,024 pounds of shot. The average fort at that time, even with the heavy 64-pounders, could usually bring at the very most ten guns to bear, or 640 pounds of shot, at a moving target. The strongest fort in Brooklyn could reply to a broadside from *Asia* with perhaps 288 pounds throw weight per volley.

Up to the time of the battle, land-based artillery had almost never won a duel with ships of the line when the ships had freedom of movement. (At the Charleston, three British ships ran aground off Fort Moultrie and were savaged by the shore batteries.) This is why Washington placed his confidence in the log booms anchored by hulks sunken in various channels. In July he noted that he "had long most religiously believed the vessel with a brisk wind and strong tide cannot, unless by chance shot, be stopped by a battery."[4]

The British, in fact, were continuously engaged in testing the American defenses. On July 12th, the British frigates *Rose* and *Phoenix,* the schooner *Tryal* and two tenders sailed up the Hudson as far as the Tappan Zee, twelve miles north of Fort Washington. In this three- by twelve-mile widening of the river they cruised with apparent indifference to the armed American presence on the shores around them, awnings stretched against the summer sun. The flotilla demonstrated its command of the sea and the Americans' inability to be masters of their own inland navigable waters by beating off a number of attacks, including one by fire boats, losing only one tender and returning to Staten Island on August 18th.

While adverse winds and tides kept the British battle fleet from cutting Brooklyn off and bombarding the inner defenses, Admiral Howe tried to provide for all contingencies. On August 7th he dispatched a small flotilla to sail around Long Island and come down the East River. This strike force of three frigates and 30 transports was held in Flushing Bay by bad weather, however, its commander unwilling to attempt the passage through Hellgate.

Following the plans for the defensive works around Brooklyn formulated by Lee and implemented, in turn, by Generals Stirling, Greene and Washington, artillery was positioned at Fort Stirling (on Brooklyn Heights, bounded today by Pierrepont, Hicks, Clark and Columbia Streets), as well as south at Red Hook — Fort Defiance — to command the northeastern approaches of the bay. As noted, a supplementary battery was placed on Governors Island across from the sea-level artillery at the Battery on Manhattan.

The landside fortifications protecting the harbor batteries on Brooklyn Neck ran a mile and a half, from the Gowanus in the south to Wallabout Bay in the north (later the site of the Brooklyn Navy Yard). The major emplacements, starting at Gowanus Creek, included the four-gun Fort Box, which commanded the Port Road. Named for General Greene's brigade major, or senior aide, Major Daniel Box, it was where Carroll Park is today. It was later called Fort Boerum. About three-quarters of a mile (or 300 rods as an 18th-century description noted) to the northeast was Fort Greene with six guns (at State and Schermerhorn Streets), and 150 yards farther to the northeast was a circular battery at what is now the corner of DeKalb and Hudson Avenues.

Fort Putnam, on the heights over Wallabout Bay, was a star-shaped battery with six cannon to secure the northern flank. Named in honor of Colonel Rufus Putnam, Israel Putnam's engineer cousin who laid out much of the fieldworks, its name was changed to Fort Greene during the War of 1812. Today, Fort Greene Park is the site of the memorial to those Americans who died in British prison ships in Wallabout Bay during the occupation. Just behind the main line of defense, at the present intersection of Atlantic Avenue and Court Street, was Cobble Hill (named by Massachusetts troops), with three guns. It was nicknamed the Corkscrew Fort after the spiral road made to move cannon to its top. In some accounts of the battle it is called Ponkiesberg by the Dutch and Bergen Hill by the English. Because it commanded the batteries on Brooklyn Heights, the British leveled it after the battle.

The command post that served as Washington's Brooklyn headquarters was set up in the Cornell House (at a spot where today's Montague Street nears the promenade in Brooklyn Heights) overlooking the ferry landing. A telegraph* was mounted on its roof for rapid communication with New York. Also, various lookouts were placed on the heights and in church steeples throughout the borough.

By the time of the battle, there were eight forts both on the harbor and the landward approaches—apart from those in Manhattan and New Jersey. Facing the water were 35 cannon ranging from 12- to 32-pounders. On the landward side were mostly 18-pound guns, which had a greater range and throw weight than the 12-pounders that composed the bulk of the British artillery in the field. Each cannon had a ready stock of 30 rounds. In all, the inner line had 28 cannon and 3,500 men at dawn on the day of the battle. More men and artillery were brought over that day and the next.

The lines were faced by a dry ditch. Trees and brushwood were cut down for over 100 yards to provide a clear field of fire for the American marksmen. A killing field was also marked off. In case of assault, the defenders were to hold their fire until the enemy had crossed a line

---

*An elevated platform for flag signals by day and lanterns by night. Perhaps this was a version of the semaphore invented by Englishman Richard Lowell Edgeworth in 1767 and named after the Greek for "I bear a sign." In its full form it was a system of visual telegraphy, signaling from watchtower to watchtower stationed five to ten miles apart.

formed by piles of brushwood placed about 50 yards from the lines. The trees cut down were made into abatis to entangle infantry much as concertina wire was used in later wars.

As well as fortifying Brooklyn Neck, the Americans occupied the three westernmost approaches, along the coast or through the passes in the hills of the Prospect Range.

In other defensive preparations, part of John Jay's earlier recommendations — that of a scorched earth policy — was carried out, to make any conquest less valuable to the enemy. The Provincial Congress ordered livestock in the endangered area to be driven east to the Hempstead Plain. Additionally, grain, hay and other stores in Brooklyn were to be moved or burned. General Woodhull with his 500-strong (on paper) Suffolk County Militia, along with some men from Queens County, was given the task. The plan was never fulfilled in its entirety, but several farmhouses, outbuildings and fields in Flatlands, New Utrecht, Flatbush and other neighboring communities were burnt by detachments of the American Army.

*   *   *

While the Americans were moving troops and munitions into the area and strengthening their fortifications, the British Army was resting on Staten Island, preparing for the battle to come. For this action, General Clinton had presented three options — all of which Howe could have exercised, considering his overwhelming strength on land and sea (although perhaps with some price to his communications).

Howe could have made a landing on Manhattan Island above the bulge where 23rd Street is today, cut the city and the American Army off from any chance of help from the outside and laid siege to New York. He could also have landed farther north on the Hudson. Before leaving for the Carolinas, Clinton, who knew New York well, had made a reconnaissance to King's Bridge, which connected Manhattan with Westchester (now the Bronx) across the Harlem Creek, and later suggested a landing at this point to isolate all of Manhattan.

As it was, and considering the difficulties presented by the forts and the boom across the Hudson at around 179th Street — well below the Harlem — Howe chose Clinton's third plan: to land at Gravesend Bay on Long Island.

Ironically, it was at this point that the first British invasion of New York (then New Amsterdam) had taken place. On August 25, 1664, Colonel Richard Nicoll, in action for the Duke of York, had landed at Gravesend, the one town founded by English settlers, to take the Dutch colony of New Netherlands.*

The choice of a landing to secure Long Island *first* may have been that of a general more interested in caution than one who preferred to gamble on one decisive action to smash the largest American army yet formed. A direct attack on Manhattan could have caused a rout of the foe, but the Americans might have escaped and re-formed on Long Island. Such a retreat would have been the Americans' best and probably only option, the East River being easier to cross than the Hudson. In addition to the Hudson's width and strong current, it would have been filled with British ships. The treacherous currents of the East River and its continually changing tides made it difficult to maintain a fleet powered by sail on station twenty-four hours a day. Small boats, however, as would later be shown, could cross it without difficulty.

Any large contingent of rebels on the Long Island, whether or not they held the artillery positions on Brooklyn Heights, added to those in Westchester and New Jersey, would confine Howe to New York, a city of 20,000 to 25,000 civilians with no ready means of supply for its citizens or his army.

General Lee, who had been sent by Washington early in the year to fortify New York, wrote to Washington on February 19th: "I wait for force to prepare a post in Long Island for three thousand men. I think this a capital object, for should the enemy take possession of New York, while Long Island is in our hands, they would find it impossible to subsist."[5]

Howe had in fact been reminded of the strategic importance of Long Island in matters of supply. It was rich in foodstuffs and fodder for the army and timber for the navy. A letter to Lord Howe published in *The Gentlemen's Magazine* noted that the island was "the only spot in

---

*The Dutch easily recaptured the colony in 1673, only to swap it the next year for Surinam (Dutch Guiana) in the Peace of Westminster.

North America for carrying on the war with efficacy against the rebels. In this fertile Island the army could subsist without any support from England or Ireland. It has a plain on it twenty-four miles long, which has a fertile country about it. Forming their camp on the above plain, they could in five or six days invade and reduce any of the Colonies at pleasure."[6]

The decision was made. A minimally opposed landing on Long Island, in part peopled by the politically neutral Dutch, would give Howe an easily defended granary to provide a source of supply to the British headquarters city.

Although, for the British, Brooklyn afforded the potential of an unopposed landing, it also provided an almost ready-made defense-in-depth for the Americans in Prospect Range, the line of hills running diagonally to the northeast from Bay Ridge, a line which resulted from the Wisconsin Glacier. Today, features of the terrain can be noted most dramatically on Lookout Hill in Prospect Park in the winter, when there is no foliage to obstruct the view. From this second-highest point in the borough one can look to the southwest and see the hills of Green-Wood Cemetery — the same as they were in the 18th century, not having been graded for city streets. To the south, Flatbush and Flatlands reflect their name, stretching without rise to the sea at Coney Island and Jamaica Bay, an outwash plain. To the north and east, the hills continue, as distinct, in a distant view, as they were at the time of the battle.

These hills offered an abrupt rampart ranging 40 to 90 feet above the plain, forming a giant natural outerworks to the inner fortifications on Brooklyn Neck in the Heights and Red Hook. The climb up Lookout Hill from its southwest side offers a good example of the difficulties of terrain the British would face, especially in late August, when dense growths of mountain laurel would compound the problems of movement. The extreme slopes of the range and the heavy foliation made the rampart impenetrable to troops in formation and to horse-drawn equipment. One unidentified contemporary writer recorded: "... to an enemy advancing from below, it presented a continuous barrier, a huge natural abattis (*sic*), impassable to artillery, where with proportionate numbers a successful defence could be sustained."[7]

To the north of this barrier, the land sloped gradually downward and was pierced by rough paths and country lanes fenced in by tall foliage and dotted by tiny clearings. It was the type of terrain that suited small units and stragglers. Certainly there were few of the large, cultivated fields and meadows common in Europe, where a major organized force would bring its superiority of numbers and firepower to bear. It was "as if designed by the Almighty to protect the defenders of Brooklyn Heights. . . . The strength of this natural position was all the greater because it overlooked a wide and open plain that extended eastward and northeastward from Gravesend Bay."[8] A British officer wrote of the north side of the moraine that it was "entirely after [the Americans'] own heart covered with woods and hedges,"[9] favoring skirmishing from covered positions and restricting the hard line of fighting the European armies preferred.

Above the Prospect Range toward Brooklyn Heights the outer line was secured by the impassable marshland of the Gowanus Creek on the Americans' right flank. North, too, of the hills lay the corridor which Atlantic Avenue now follows and which was, and is, flat hard land. This corridor contained the Jamaica Road, running almost parallel to the hills, the key channel for resupply of the outlying American detachments and an ideal route for a controlled fighting withdrawal to the inner lines.

Farther north, on the left flank of the inner defenses, was additional swampy terrain that extended from Wallabout Bay to Newtown Creek, where Grand and Flushing Avenues now lie. In all, Washington had two strong, easily defended lines and the advantage of a good internal network of roads for rapid resupply and reinforcement.

* * *

In the battle to come, there were at least 32 generals whose names were recorded, an average of one for each 1,200 men. Communications on the field of battle were by word of mouth, orders being carried by courier — or signaled by flag and drumbeat and, in the cavalry, by hunting horn. To be effective in action, generals had to be close to the scene. In such battles, before electronic communications, controlling units in the field required a higher percentage of officers than in a modern army. However, not all of the generals were exclusively field commanders. Armies were growing in size and complexity and the face of war was beginning to change dramatically.

Previously, a general commanding had his aides who more or less handled staff duties as the need arose. Washington's aides were called his "family" and were supposed to stay close to the General and be ready for duty twenty-four hours a day. By the time of the Battle of Brooklyn, British and American forces having grown to the tens of thousands, staff work was beginning to be organized and duties codified. On the day of the battle, Major General James Robertson was Howe's administrative aide as well as a commander in the field, and General Thomas Mifflin acted as Washington's Quartermaster General with duties shared by Colonel Stephen Moylan.

During this era the quartermaster was responsible for logistics at its widest definition — everything from clothing, housing and feeding the army to organizing troop movements. The position originated in France as major general "*des logis*"; hence, the word "logistics." In the French Army a major general was not a rank but a position, chief of staff. In Germany it became *Quartiermeister*. In theory, Mifflin and Moylan should have handled all the housekeeping and organizational duties, leaving Washington free to command the army. In reality, it was not until later in the war that Washington had an experienced staff to relieve him of the petty details that interfered with his prime responsibilities.

On the British side, William Howe would benefit from a more experienced and efficient supply and administrative structure. Directly under him were Lieutenant Generals Clinton and Cornwallis. Lord Percy, also a Lieutenant General, commanded the cavalry. Other British generals included: Major Generals Pigott, Agnew, Smith, Vaughn, Grant, Mathews and Jones; Brigadier Generals Leslie, Cleveland and Erskine. Lieutenant General de Heister commanded the Hessian contingent with, as division chiefs, Major Generals von Mirbach and von Stirn. General Robertson, as noted, acted in a staff capacity to Howe.

Israel Putnam would be Washington's commander on Long Island, with Sullivan, Stirling and Parsons commanding the forces on the advanced lines. Behind the earthworks surrounding the village of Brooklyn, in various command and staff positions, were Generals Mifflin, Spencer, Fellows, Heard, Wadsworth, McDougal and Scott (the latter a firebrand lawyer appointed to lead the New York Militia, though there is no record of his exercising command of troops during the battle).

The initial commander charged with planning the battle, Nathanael Greene, had envisioned an elastic defense, seeking to savage the British in the passes. After the first bloodletting, the plan anticipated the British wasting themselves in pursuit along the Atlantic Avenue corridor and being stopped at the inner fortifications. Greene's successors, especially Sullivan and Putnam, had no cogent battle plan other than to fight on the spot and win. They had apparently given no thought to war objectives, political considerations or contingency scenarios. Washington, in overall command, had delegated the operations in Brooklyn to subordinates. By the time of the battle, Washington was occupied in New York by housekeeping duties — getting the army ready, in place and securing munitions and provisions — jobs normally attended to by a staff.

CHAPTER VII

"Be cool, but determined; do not fire at a distance..."

O N THURSDAY, AUGUST 22ND, the British fleet was on the move, crossing the mile-and-an-eighth-wide Narrows under cover of the guns of the frigates *Rose, Phoenix, Rainbow* and *Greyhound*. *Rainbow* was stationed just north of Denyse ferry landing to provide enfilading fire up the Shore Road, should it be used to reinforce the Americans at the landing site. Two bomb ketches, *Thunder* and *Carcass,* were on hand to counter cannon fire from the ridge above.

Admiral Howe detailed the frigates to provide covering fire for the landing both to silence any American artillery and to support a march north along the shore should the opportunity arise. In the New York theater, Howe had some 23 frigates under his command, two ships of the line (men-of-war), and a great number of sloops, cutters, bomb ketches and one schooner, as well as transport barges for the troops.

Frigates were the cruisers of the time and the workhorses of the sailing navy. They carried 20 to 50 guns, were fast sailers and had a high level of endurance at sea. They usually were not the focus of great sea battles between fleets, however, as this work was handled by the men-of-war, or ships of the (fighting) line. These carried 52 or more guns at a higher rate of gunnage to displacement than did the frigates. Because of the weight of the guns and shot (in the case of the 64-gun *Asia*, about 360,000 pounds in cannon and at least 65,000 pounds for the minimum load of shot) and provisions needed for the larger crew and complement of marines, the men-of-war were low-endurance vessels. They could only remain at sea for a relatively short period of time before needing resupply from a naval dockyard.

The smallest fighting ships of the period were sloops-of-war and armed cutters, mounting 10 to 18 guns. The only distinction was that the sloop had a fixed bowsprit. Either were fast and were used for patrolling, picket and signal duties. Additionally, in Howe's arsenal were the bomb ketches — small, slow-moving boats often towed into place and anchored, which mounted one or more mortars (short-barrelled cannon with a high trajectory that could lob solid or exploding shot over the walls of a fortification).

Any of these ships-of-war could provide covering fire for ground forces, even to neutralizing enemy emplacements on heights overlooking the water simply by elevating the muzzles of their cannon or tilting the ship by shifting weight on board, or waiting for the right wave to gain trajectory. Land-based artillery had problems firing on close-in ships due to gravity; they could not depress the cannon barrels because the shot would roll out.

The British had used their time spent on Staten Island to construct the small boats needed for the crossing. The majority of these were basically rafts with high gunwales, perfectly adequate in calm weather for the job of moving thousands of soldiers and their equipment. For the initial assault on the beachhead, however, the British had built landing craft — boats with hinged, flat bows which on landing could be let down to form ramps for rapid unloading. These were much like the Landing Craft Infantry (LCI) of the Second World War.

The troops designated to assault the beaches crossed tightly packed, seated in the boats; their weapons, loaded and with bayonets fixed, were between their knees. When this mini-armada was a few hundred yards from the beach, Commodore William Hotham on the leading boat broke out a red flag to signal the craft to deploy into lines ten abreast. According to a Captain Duncan: "... in ten minutes or less, four thousand men were on the beach, formed and ready to move forward."[1]

The British came ashore at the site of Denyse ferry, now Fort Hamilton in New Utrecht, and farther south, at Gravesend Bay. On the heights overlooking the Narrows, Washington had posted Colonel

Edward Hand with 200 Pennsylvania riflemen. After peppering the oncoming boats with a few shots, Hand withdrew, burning supplies and what forage crops he could find on his way north. One Hessian officer commented on the ease of the operation as well as the earlier landing from the transport fleet on Staten Island: "When we disembarked on Staten Island, they might have destroyed a good many of our people with two six-pounders, and now [on Long Island] they might have made it very nasty for us."[2]

That morning, General Washington was still uncertain of Howe's plans, having received reports of only 9,000 men crossing to Brooklyn. Still believing this was a feint, and that Howe might probe in some strength directly up the coast, he reinforced the troops in Brooklyn with only six regiments, keeping back half his forces to counter the attacks he still expected on Manhattan Island.

First to secure the beachhead were a corps of Jaegers and Hessian Grenadiers with 40 cannon under Colonel Emil Count von Donop and two battalions of light infantry and six field pieces commanded by General Cornwallis. "At Daybreak Reserve embarked in flatboats," wrote Stephen Kemble, General Howe's adjutant, "towed to Long Island & landed about 9 A.M. at New Utrecht, without the smallest opposition. The ships with the rest of the troops came all ashore by twelve, 14,700 men."[3] In all, there were 75 flatboats and galleys, and eleven bateaux, used for the landing.

That afternoon, the 17th Regiment of Light Dragoons, units of the British Grenadiers and more artillery and Hessians came over. These marched to DeBruynnes Land, today 21st Avenue, and along the King's Highway, reaching as far as what is West First Street. This latest shipment of Hessians was a corps of 5,000 under Lieutenant General Leopold Philip de Heister; Baron Wilhelm von Knyphausen was second in command. General de Heister proudly recalled the Hessians standing at attention with "sloped" (shouldered) arms on their flatboats, as they crossed and landed, moving inland "in column of march, preserving the well-considered pomp of German disciplin (*sic*)."[4]

Kemble continued: "The Advance under Lt. Gen. Clinton and Earl Cornwallis, the reserve composed of Grenadiers of the 42nd & 33rd Regts. with part of the Light Infantry, proceeded immediately to

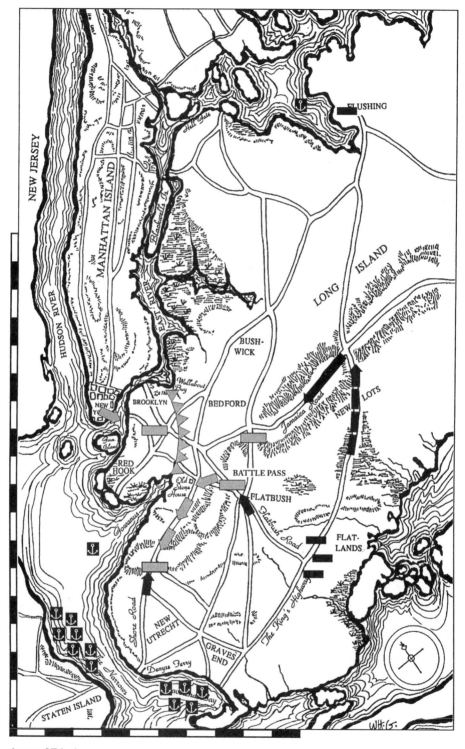

August 27th, 4 a.m.

Flatbush with 1,500 Hessians under Col. Donop where they had some skirmishing with the Rebels from the Heights leading to Brookland Ferry & a few men were killed & wounded, but of no consequence. Part of the Light Infantry & the 71st [Brigade] took post at Flatlands Church. The rest of our army extending from Gravesend to New Utrecht remained in position until the 26th, at night when they were ordered to march."[5]

That first night the winds increased in force, making the channel hazardous for small boats, and so the ferrying of additional troops was stopped. The British had secured positions up to two miles from the beachhead and there was no reason to risk losing one or more of the flatboats loaded with soldiers, each strapped into as much as 120 pounds of equipment. The remainder of the invasion force did not cross until the day before the battle.

Immediately on securing the beachhead, Cornwallis marched to Flatbush and sent out patrols toward the Flatbush and Bedford Passes, probing the outer defenses. These were light infantry, the German Jaegers, fast-moving, lightly encumbered and trained for reconnaissance in force.

The next morning there was some fighting heard from the Shore Road. To back up General Grant's forces and prevent an American push on this route, the frigates *Roebuck* and *Repulse* were dispatched to bombard the American forts and cut off American traffic across the East River. The winds and tides were adverse and only the lighter *Roebuck* could "fetch up high enough to the northward to exchange a few random shots with the battery on Red Hook," Howe reported.[6] He learned later that the random shots had knocked out the battery.

On Friday morning a battalion of 550 Pennsylvania riflemen under Colonel Hand attacked the Hessian encampment in Flatbush. The Germans could only repel the attack by calling up artillery. The next day, the 24th, the Americans again attacked, burning houses that belonged to Jeremiah Vanderbilt, Everts Hegeman and Leffert Lefferts. On Sunday, the 25th, some of the Pennsylvanians dragged a few pieces of artillery to the edge of the woods and opened fire on the Hessians, who, even with supporting artillery, had great difficulty beating off this latest attack.

Washington's Adjutant General, Joseph Reed, wrote to his wife on the 24th from New York:

> Our troops have been skirmishing with the enemy on L.I. with various fortune, but we have generally driven them back; several were killed on both sides. Most of the Penn. troops are ordered over. The officers and men behave exceedingly well, and the whole army is in better spirits than I have known it at any time. The gallantry of the southern [Pennsylvania] men has inspired all others, so that there will be an emulation who shall behave best. There is a wood between our works and the enemy's camp of which each party is endeavoring to possess themselves. As yet we have kept it, and hope we shall, as it is very important. The enemy's ships are moving so much downwards, that we begin to think their grand attack will be on Long Island. Indeed, the city is now so strong that in the present temper of our men, the enemy would lose half their army in attempting to take it. While I am writing (late on Saturday) there is a heavy firing and clouds of smoke rising from that wood. . . ."[7]

"The Rebels approached twice, fired howitzers and used grape and ball so that all our artillery had to come up," one Hessian officer wrote. "At noon I slept a little while, and was waked by two cannonballs which covered me with earth."[8]

Washington was in Brooklyn on the 24th, examining the ground and the works. When he returned to New York late that afternoon he gave the command in Brooklyn to Israel Putnam. "General Putnam was made happy by obtaining leave to go over. The old man was quite miserable at being kept here," wrote Joseph Reed.[9]

With Putnam went Washington's observations and instructions, urging him to devote only his best troops to the front lines and keep the militia behind the main fortifications. "The militia," Washington directed, "or the most indifferent troops will do for the interior works; whilst your best men should at all hazards prevent the enemy's passing the woods and approaching your works."[10]

Putnam also brought a Major Aaron Burr as part of his staff, who, it is said, conducted himself admirably in the battle and the evacuation.

Burr's later rival, Alexander Hamilton, was a captain in the Provincial Company of New York Artillery, and during the battle was in command of the redoubt on Bayard's Hill in lower Manhattan.

The skirmishing going on, the unexpected and persistent attacks, were not in the rule book for continental warfare between the great armies of Europe, and this distressed the Hessians. The nature of the attacks, the inflated estimate of the number of Americans facing them, the vague mystery of the dark forests, swamps and thickets—perhaps calling up images of ogres and trolls in a suggestible Teutonic mind— plus their knowledge that the Americans had been issued tomahawks all combined to appall the Hessians. The Germans, then, were greatly relieved early on Monday the 26th, while fighting off yet another attack by the zealous Pennsylvanians, to receive orders from Cornwallis to withdraw to the major British positions.

However harassing these assaults were to the enemy, they were met with disfavor by Washington (and scorn by the Hessian officer whose sleep was disturbed). Washington scolded Putnam in a letter on the 25th: "I perceived yesterday, a scattering, unmeaning and wasteful fire from our people at the enemy, a kind of fire which tended to disgrace our men as soldiers and rend our defence contemptible in the eyes of the enemy."[11]

In addition to alluding to Putnam's lack of control over his command, Washington saw these impromptu skirmishes as wastes of ammunition that also tended to frighten off any of the enemy who might be thinking of deserting. But worst of all, these miscellaneous attacks, not cleared with headquarters, made it impossible to distinguish between a real or a false alarm of the beginning of the enemy's expected main thrust.

Washington intended that there be specifically directed probes to keep the enemy off guard and possibly bring back prisoners and intelligence. He did not want the freelance harassment that Putnam had found to work against isolated Indian parties and villages in earlier wars.

The Hessian officer cited also wrote: "[The rebels] have some very good marksmen, but some of them have wretched guns, and most of them shoot crooked. But they are clever at hunter's wiles. They climb trees, they crawl forward on their bellies for one hundred and fifty paces, shoot, and go as quickly back again. They make themselves shelters of boughs, etc. But today they are much put out by our greencoats [Jaegers] for we don't let our fellows fire unless they can get good aim at a man, so that they dare not undertake anything more against us."[12]

For the civilian population, uncertainties over British plans could be unsettling. Even the strange weather panicked some. What might be assumed as prolonged heat thunder started an exodus of the locals inland, while the British were still on Staten Island.

In the mid-19th century a Brooklynite, Judge Furman, recorded stories told him by his aunt about the battle:

> . . . on the second or third day before the landing of the British troops upon Long Island, an apparent cannonading was heard. So very distinct was this cannonading, and so very regular was it and continuous, that all the inhabitants of the island residing between the distance of two miles from the city of New York and about thirty-five miles down the island, were satisfied that the British had landed and attacked the American army. Those residing to the west end of the island immediately commenced moving their families and driving their cattle towards the interior and in such numbers, that my aunt Tyler, then a young girl, and living at her home in New Lots, nine miles from Brooklyn ferry, tells me she was awakened the next morning by the lowing of cattle, and upon arising, she found the roads blocked up with cows, horses, sheep, &c., which had been driven up during the night to escape the plunder of the British, as they supposed. In the morning, however, it was discovered that the British army had not stirred a foot from their encampment on Staten Island, and that not a single cannon had been fired! The next day after — as if, indeed, it had been intended by a good Providence as a warning to the people of what was fast approaching — the roads between the city of New York and Jamaica, nine miles distant, were covered with the British light horsemen, in their scarlet cloaks."[13]

During the four days preceding the battle, the fears of Brooklynites grew in anticipation of barbarity on the part of the foreigners — meaning Hessians and New Englanders alike. Among the Dutch there was a genuine dislike and distrust for New Englanders — particularly those from Connecticut. Originally, the colony of New Netherlands had included all of Long Island and extended as far east as the Connecticut River. Sharp dealings by the New Englanders had whittled this territory down, in the Dutch view, even before geopolitics had taken a hand. A common tale of advancing British parties and American patrols was of finding food on the tables of abandoned Dutch farmhouses, each side suspecting it to be poisoned by the other.

Because Washington had a better idea of Howe's intentions after his visit to Brooklyn on the 23rd, on the 24th and 25th he moved more troops across the East River. Convinced on his inspection on the 26th that Howe's big push would indeed take place in Brooklyn, he then brought over as many reinforcements as he could spare from Manhattan.

During these days, smoke and flames appeared in the sky, but it was not known whether this was part of the Continental Congress' scorched earth policy, or some unfathomable action on the part of the British invaders. And, to a previously verdant and pastoral scene, the sounds of military preparations, the drums and martial music, and the sight of the white tents of thousands of invaders tinged the atmosphere. The collected combatants outnumbered the residents of Brooklyn by about fifteen to one.

*   *   *

On Friday, after consolidating the British beachhead, General Howe, once more in his role as peacemaker, issued his second proclamation,[14] from the farmhouse of Denyse Denyse. It offered forgiveness and protection:

> Whereas it is reported that many of the loyal inhabitants of this Island have been compelled by the leaders of the rebellion to take up arms against his Majesty's government, notice is hereby given to all persons so forced into rebellion, that on delivering themselves up at the Headquarters of the Army, they will be recognized as faithful subjects having permission peaceably to return to their respective dwellings and to meet with full protection for persons and property. All who choose to take up arms for the

restoration of order and Good Government within this Island, shall be disposed of in the best manner and have every encouragement that can be expected.

Given under hand and seal, at Head Quarters, Long Island: August 23rd, 1776   William Howe

Howe might have had a more informed perspective on the determination of his opponents if he had heard Washington's own proclamation, given the following day. On Saturday, the 24th, when Washington visited and inspected the interior defenses in Brooklyn, he exhorted the troops:

> The enemy have now landed on Long Island, and the hour is fast approaching in which the honor and success of this army, and the safety of our bleeding country, will depend. Remember, officers and soldiers, that you are freemen, fighting for the blessings of liberty, and slavery will be your portion, if you do not acquit yourselves like men. Remember how your courage and spirit have been despised and traduced by your cruel invaders, though they have found by dear experience at Boston, Charlestown, and other places, what a few brave men, contending in their own land, and in the best of causes can do against hirelings and mercenaries. . . . Those who are distinguished for their gallantry and good conduct may depend on being honorably noticed and suitably rewarded; and if this army will but emulate and imitate their brave countrymen in other parts of America, [the commander] has no doubt they will, by glorious victory, save their country, and acquire to themselves immortal honor.[15]

Washington also offered advice, and a warning: "Be cool, but determined; do not fire at a distance, but wait for orders from your officers. It is the general's express orders, that if any man attempt to skulk, lie down, or retreat without orders, he be instantly shot down as an example. . . ."[16]

CHAPTER VIII

"Across these hills...
the nearest way to Gowanus"

TO MOUNT THEIR ATTACK, the British had five possible routes through the hills to the fortifications around Brooklyn Neck. From the shoreline to the east these were: (1) the Shore Road following the curve of the bay; (2) Martense Pass, through what is now the southern end of Green-Wood Cemetery, joining the Shore Road at the Gowanus just south of where the Vechte-Cortelyou (Old Stone) House now stands; (3) Flatbush Pass, near today's Zoo in Prospect Park; (4) Bedford Pass through the Flatlands, today at the intersection of Bedford and Rodgers Avenues; and (5) east along the King's Highway to a small settlement just beginning to be known as the New Lots and on through Jamaica Pass in today's Evergreen Cemetery.

As it was, Howe chose the Jamaica Pass for a wide-ranging movement around the American defenses. Henry Clinton was the author of the plan: a cohesive, well-thought-out strategy, a grand version of the simple expedient learned when men first fought with weapons in their right hands: to roll up the enemy's weaker left flank. It was based on excellent intelligence, something the Americans had neglected, in part because they were occupied with the almost overwhelming task of fielding and supplying a large new army in the first place.

One can easily assume the British knew more about the terrain than the Americans. Many British officers had served in the city or visited it. Clinton himself was born in New York; his father was Royal Governor of the Province. In the several months preceding August 1776, Clinton had made a critical reconnaissance of the area. Lieutenant Colonel Kemble, Howe's aide, was a member of the 60th Royal Americans, stationed on Governors Island until only a short time before the troubles came to a head. Most of the British officers who had passed through the province had been to Jamaica and Hempstead in social visits and they would have taken a professional interest in the terrain they passed through.

Further, the Loyalists were constantly sending information across the lines to Howe concerning the American dispositions, both physical and political. And the main route for young men from New England seeking to join the British forces was across Long Island Sound and through the Jamaica Pass to wait on the shores of Jamaica Bay for a British boat to take them to Staten Island. These volunteers would certainly have been questioned on what they had seen. Indeed, British ships regularly delivered supplies of gunpowder and weapons to Loyalists on Long Island — and in one case a cannon came with its own Royal Navy instructor.* The boats would return with valuable information.

Additionally, the British had what would later be called "agents" in place, merchants or tradesmen who through simple loyalty to the Crown or for mercantile advantage maintained regular correspondence with those in power and, in times of need, communicated tactical information directly to the British forces. These agents were objective, experienced reporters. The information they provided was, for the most part, valuable and could be confirmed by that of other sources.

The American Army, for its part, had only the barest knowledge of the island on which it found itself, and at best slight information

---

*As early as November 30, 1775, the ship of the line *Asia* had anchored off Long Beach to deliver a supply of small arms, ammunition and a six-pound cannon complete with a Royal Navy gunner. Loyalist Richard Hewlett, who received the munitions, was told to hide them in preparation for the conflict to come. Viewing the cannon as his personal property, however, he took it with him in his military travels around Long Island with the Loyalist company he had formed, and later in his command of the Third Battalion of DeLancey's Brigade, created in September 1776. The gun remained behind in 1783 when Hewlett left for Nova Scotia and now rests in the backyard of a house in Cold Spring Harbor once owned by him.

about the forces arrayed against it. They knew little of the British order of battle—their units and their strength. Apart from forays by Pennsylvania units that were more concerned with harassing their enemies than with bringing back intelligence, there seemed to be no reconnaissance. And the few Whig families communicating with the American forces either told wild stories about the size of the army opposing them or brought small pieces of information that the Americans were unable to process due to lack of organization. Local commanders neither passed information up to an officer or staff responsible for intelligence, nor were they debriefed. Both were practices of the British, however much in rudimentary form, with the information shared in daily conferences.

General Greene, who made it a point to scout out the terrain during the months he was in charge in Brooklyn, had been invalided to the reaches of Long Island and was unavailable to lend his experience. And Generals Sullivan and Putnam, in command for only a short time before the action, had not even visited the outerworks of the defense. To his credit, Sullivan claimed to have paid from his own pocket for a number of vedettes (mounted sentries), if not to make a reconnaissance, at least to warn of any enemy movement toward the American lines from the undefended left flank. As it turned out, this paid service did not operate when needed.

In the days prior to the attack, Howe let it be known, and maneuvered his troops to give the impression, that he would attack on the western sector and avoid the presumed long and difficult sweep to the east and the Jamaica Pass.

On his visit to Brooklyn on the 26th, Washington inspected the inner and other fortifications and gathered as much information about British dispositions as he could. This was the visit after which he started pouring troops into Brooklyn from Manhattan. While it is said what he observed "gave him great anxiety,"[1] Washington told his aides on retiring that night: "The same Providence that rules to-day will rule to-morrow, gentlemen. Good-night."[2]

The Americans had fortified all the routes through the hills but the easternmost, on the Jamaica Road. On the eve of the battle, the American left was hanging in the air, defended by a corporal's guard.

To remedy this lapse, on Monday, the day before the battle, Washington ordered Colonel Samuel Miles and about 500 riflemen to patrol toward the Jamaica Pass.

In retrospect, a light cavalry* squadron would have slowed any British advance from this direction and given the defenders more of a chance to turn and face the enemy thrust. In June, Connecticut had sent Washington three cavalry regiments, called light horse, totaling about 400 men. Either Washington was totally ignorant of the uses of cavalry — or mounted infantry — or he was overwhelmed by the problems of the feeding and care of a large number of animals. He had earlier expressed skepticism over the value of cavalry and wanted to use the Connecticut contingent dismounted as infantry, sending the horses to Westchester for later use as officer remounts or as dray animals. When the Connecticut Light Horse demurred, he dismissed them. Washington wrote their commander: "They can no longer be of use here, where horse cannot be brought into action, and I do not care how soon they are dismissed."[3]

Washington had enough difficulties feeding his men and what horses he did have. At 20 pounds per animal, he might have felt that an additional 8,000 pounds of forage a day was beyond the capabilities of his supply structure. While horses do need supplementary food, however — oats or wheat in the winter months — there was plenty of high-quality forage, grass and a profusion of meadows behind the outer defenses in Brooklyn that rainy summer, and particularly around the Jamaica Pass.

Had Washington kept this force in being, it could have been used to create havoc behind the British lines. In smaller parties it could have provided valuable information through patrols and, on the day of the battle, a potentially decisive flying column of skirmishers against Howe's flanking movement.

On that Monday, with the armies separated by the line of wooded hills, Putnam could field perhaps 7,000 effective troops, including those

---

*Lacking a history of feudal warfare, the United States has never had the traditional armored, or heavy, cavalry, such as the French cuirassiers or the British Household Cavalry.

manning the inner fortifications. His right wing was secured by the salt marshes of the Gowanus; his left (as he considered it), a mile or two away, by detachments holding the Flatbush and Bedford Passes.

*   *   *

On Monday evening, August 26th, the British began their move. The left wing, under Major General James Grant, was ready to push up the coast.

An officer in Colonel Atlee's battalion (which had been teamed with Hand's Pennsylvania Regiment) recorded: "Yesterday (Monday) about 120 of our men went as a guard to a place on Long Island called Red Lion; about eleven at night the sentries described two men coming up a water-melon patch, upon which our men fired on them. The enemy then retreated, and about one o'clock advanced with 200 or 300 men, and endeavored to surround our guard, but they being watchful, gave them two or three fires, and retreated to alarm the remainder of the battalion, except one lieutenant and about fifteen men who have not been heard of as yet. About four o'clock this morning, the alarm was given by beating to arms, when the remainder of our battalions, went to the place our men retreated from. About a quarter of a mile this side we saw the enemy, when we got into the woods (our battalion being the advanced guard) amidst the incessant fire of their field-pieces loaded with grape-shot, which continued till ten o'clock. . . ."[4]

"Last Monday we went over to L.I.," wrote an American rifleman, "and about midnight were alarmed by some of our scouting parties, who advised us that the enemy were coming up the Island with several field-pieces. Upon which near 3,000 men were ordered out, chiefly of Marylanders and Pennsylvanians, to attack them on their march. About sunrise we came up with a large body of them. The Delaware and Maryland battalion made one part. Col. Atlee, with his battalion, a little before us, had taken post in an orchard, and behind a barn; and on the approach of the enemy he gave them a very severe fire for a considerable time, till they were nearly surrounding him, when he retreated to the woods. The enemy then advanced to us, when Lord Stirling, who commanded, immediately drew up in a line, and offered them battle in the true English taste."[5]

This was the first point of contact and it was not in the plans. Around 10 P.M. that Monday, some British troopers were foraging for watermelon near the Red Lion Inn. The tavern catered to tourists, who came to see what was said to be the Devil's hoofprint in a rock; the watermelon patch was planted as a further attraction to visitors. The foragers stumbled into a party from Colonel Hand's Pennsylvania Regiment near Martense Lane, just below where today's 39th Street meets Fifth Avenue.

This accidental meeting had played into British hands. Howe wanted the Americans to believe the major push was to be along the Gowanus Road. If Washington committed the majority of his command to fighting Grant, then it would be trapped between converging forces. The chance meeting had become a major firefight by dawn and it raged across a quarter-mile front, from between 38th and 39th Streets from near Second to about Fifth Avenues on today's maps. So intense was the firing that Grant, in his enthusiasm to create the illusion that the battle would take place along the coast, used up his anticipated daily battle load of ammunition and needed to bring up an emergency resupply.

As even in this day of urban noise, summer fireworks on the East River can be heard five miles away in Brooklyn, so could Grant's bombardment be heard in New York. As he expected, Washington woke early that morning to the "deep thunder of distant cannon."[6]

The second British thrust — in the center along the Flatbush Road — was composed of Hessians and Scots under General de Heister. These two pushes were feints to keep the Americans occupied while Howe maneuvered behind them.

Leaving its campfires burning to disguise its intentions, the British right wing, some 14,000 strong, moved north and east, following King's Highway to the New Lots. After flanking the outer line of defenses they were to turn to the west, successively hitting the American positions at the Bedford and Battle Passes and on the Gowanus with overwhelming force. Commanded by General Howe in person, it was the largest of the three attacking corps and composed of the most experienced units of the army. Clinton commanded the advance, a corps of light infantry, who, under cover of night, were to move carefully, sawing fallen trees that blocked the way, lest the sound of axes give warning.

Interestingly enough, even in 1776 in the wilds of eastern Brooklyn and in the dead of night people were to be expected: farmers in the outlying reaches of the county would make the overnight trip with their carts over the rutted paths to take the dawn ferry to the market in Manhattan. Then, there were those who would linger at a crossroads tavern and find their way home in the middle of the night. British orders were that travelers encountered during the maneuver were to be arrested and held until after the battle.

By 9 P.M., in the light of the full moon, the column was on the move. The point was taken by the Right Light Infantry, a unit trained to move rapidly through difficult terrain made more hazardous by the darkness. The main body under Hugh Earl Percy consisted of the Grenadiers of the 33rd West Riding, the Grenadiers of the 42nd Guards, the First Brigade, the 71st Highlanders, and the Second, Third and Fifth Brigades. The 17th Light Dragoons provided cavalry support and there were ten light field pieces. Cornwallis followed at the rear with four 12-pound cannon, the 49th Regiment and the baggage train with another 14 guns. In all, the column was over two miles long. Further, the British had learned well the lessons of earlier wars in America. To protect against surprise attacks, each segment of the column had its own flankers and skirmishing party.

The British allowed themselves 12 hours to make their way over the five miles to the Jamaica Pass and the three miles more to Bedford Village by 9 A.M., when, according to plan, all three columns would attack in unison. Howe's intelligence suggested the two choke points on his route — spots whose geography made them easily defended by a few against a much larger force — were lightly, if at all, defended. These points were Schoonmaacher's Bridge over Goose Creek, just below the boundary of East New York, and the Jamaica Pass. William Howard, Jr., the son of the owner of the Rising Sun Tavern, recalled: "The information Lord (*sic*) Howe had received by his [Tory] guides from New Utrecht. . . was exceedingly accurate."[7]

No matter how good the intelligence might have been, the column exercised great watchfulness, constantly expecting to be fired upon, their astonishment growing as they found more of the way unguarded. According to Howard: ". . . the British officers were apprehensive that

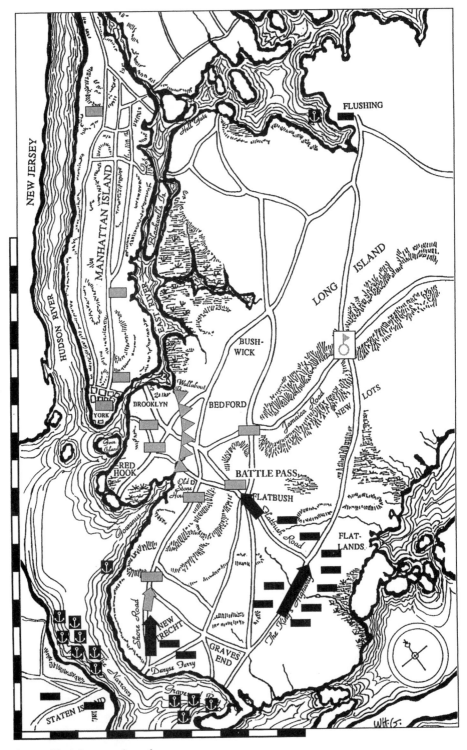

August 22nd, 9 a.m. to late afternoon

the American forces had been withdrawn only to be concentrated upon
some other point where their attack would be made under great
advantage, and [the British] loss be very heavy."[8]

The light infantry reached the bridge and were surprised to find no
resistance. The route to the Jamaica Road was free. At midnight the head
of the column reached the turnpike at the intersection of today's
Broadway and Jamaica Avenue, a small settlement around the Rising
Sun Tavern. Here, they waited quietly in the woods as the rest of the
force moved up, and until the last of the market carts rumbled off toward
New York and the lights in the tavern went out.

At 2:00 A.M., soldiers with fixed bayonets surrounded the other
houses in the settlement to prevent the spread of alarm to the Americans.
A party of soldiers accompanied by the four generals, Howe, Cornwallis,
Clinton and Percy, broke into the tavern. William Howard, and his wife
and son, William Jr., were roused from bed and taken to Howe.
According to the son:

> General Howe and another officer were standing in the bar room.
> General Howe wore a camlet [rough herringbone tweed] cloak
> over his regimentals. After asking for a glass of liquor from the
> bar, which was given him, he entered into familiar conversation
> with my father, and among other things said: "I must have
> someone of you show me over the Rockaway Path around the
> Pass."
>
> My father replied: "We belong to the other side, General,
> and can't serve you against our duty." General Howe replied:
> "That is all right — stick to your country, or stick to your princi-
> ples, but, Howard, you are my prisoner, and must guide my men
> over the hill." My father made some further objection, but was
> silenced by the General, who said: "You have no alternative. If
> you refuse, I shall have you shot through the head."
>
> Lord Howe inquired minutely about the road through the
> hills, and the position of the American guard, supposed by him
> occupying that place. So assured was he of the presence there of
> a strong force, it appearing so incredible that so favorable a
> position for resisting his passage should not be occupied, that he
> did not take the precaution of sending out his scouts to ascertain
> the fact. My father, thus compelled to serve the cause of the

enemy, was marched out under a guard, who had orders to shoot him if he attempted to desert, and I was taken along with him . . ."9*

The moon had set by 3:00 A.M. In the total darkness of the forest the two Howards led the British along an obscure trail over the hills, east of the tavern to a point flanking the pass. It was the last choke point, one Howe assumed must be heavily guarded. Howard's son recalled: "The pioneers came just behind us, and sawed down the trees which came in the way of the cannon, as the noise made by felling them with axes, it was expected, would alarm the American guard. This force was supposed to be stationed in the hills about a quarter of a mile from the tavern near where the Toll House on the Brooklyn and Jamaica turnpike stands."11

As it turned out, this last major obstacle was lightly guarded. During the few days he was in overall charge in Brooklyn, General Sullivan had felt uneasy about the lack of defenses on his left wing, east of Bedford Village. He wrote: "[I] had paid horsemen fifty dollars for patrolling it by night while I had command, as I had no foot for the purpose."12 These five vedettes, a group of officers, not a regular mounted patrol, were still on duty the night of the attack. They had been on the alert for five days, however, and were careless that night. They gave some minor resistance but were easily captured.

As various contingents moved up through the pass and occupied the Bushwick hills, the British regrouped and had their early meal. This last passage had been the hilliest of the march. The cannon, mediums of 12-pound bore weighing in total at least 1,200 pounds and normally drawn by four horses, had to be pulled up the slope by six at a full gallop.

---

*Although Howard's son dictated the story more than 70 years after the event, and his memory may have been clouded, I have chosen to use his version as, after all, he was an eyewitness. Still, the fact that Howe was wearing a civilian hat and tweed traveling cloak lends credence to another story recorded earlier than Howard's. In this version, Howe, Clinton and two other men entered the tavern, ordered a drink and asked Howard if he was a member of the "Association" — meaning was he in favor of the rebellion? When Howard answered yes, Howe drew a pistol from under his cloak and said: "That's all very well — stick to your integrity. But now you are my prisoner, and must lead me across these hills out of the way of the enemy, the nearest way to Gowanus."10

The column continued on to Bedford to wait until 9 A.M., when they would sound the signal guns for the general attack.

The British troops had been on the alert, their adrenaline flowing throughout the night. In the van, they were concerned with meeting the enemy in force—for the narrow track hemmed in by heavy foliage would prevent them from using their superiority of numbers. Along the column there was fear of a surprise attack by an enemy who was capable of melting into the dark forest. This constant tension, the physical exertion of an all-night march, the rough footing and muddy pools of the rutted path, the enforced silence, the stops and starts of marching in any column—eight miles in ten or twelve hours—had taken its toll on the men's nerves.

Captain Sir James Murray, 57th Regiment, in the forward part of the column, recalled: "[The march was] as disagreeable a one as I remember to have passed in the course of my campaigning. . . . We dragged on at the most tedious pace from sunset till 3 o'clock in the morning, halting every minute just long enough to drop asleep and to be disturbed again in order to proceed twenty yards in the same manner. The night was colder too than I remember to have felt it, so that by daybreak my stock of patience had begun to run very low."[13]

It was about 5:30 A.M. with the sun rising when the British started arriving in Bedford, the jumping-off position for the attack. Relief surged through the ranks. To quote historian Henry Stiles: ". . . the profound silence and secrecy which had previously characterized their movements, gave way to a feeling of exultant joy. They felt assured that the great object of their long and wary night-march was fully accomplished." When the order to advance was given, "their bands struck up lively strains of martial music, and, with elastic step, the troops pressed eagerly forward towards Brooklyn."[14]

CHAPTER IX

"If I see any man turn his back today, I will shoot him through"

THE BRITISH STEAMROLLER bearing down was designed primarily to outflank the Americans and convince them to surrender without too many casualties on either side. Regardless of bloodlust on the part of individual soldiers to deal violently with the rebellious "banditti," as Howe's adjutant had earlier termed the Americans, the British government did not easily field such a large expeditionary army, and had no wish to see it mangled in a large-scale battle. It was a plan in the grand tradition of 18th-century warfare to very sensibly maneuver the foe into an untenable position and then ask for surrender—which was usually given. This is what happened at the siege of Yorktown when Washington and Rochambeau outnumbered and surrounded Cornwallis. Seeing the futility of fighting, Cornwallis surrendered his sword.

At the Battle of Brooklyn, the Americans chose to stand and fight, despite the odds.

As the sun rose on August 27th, ". . . 17,000 of the best troops of Europe met 5,500 undisciplined men in the first pitched battle of the Revolution,"[1] one observer commented. And others, who watched the British from rooftops in Manhattan or from their farmhouses in Brooklyn, were awe-stricken. Howe's army, it seemed, contained more men than any had ever seen. The Redcoats marched by in never-ending lines; the polished shields on the helmets of the Hessians looked like sheets of fire in the sunlight.

On receiving news of the skirmishing at the watermelon patch, Israel Put.am first rode to alert Stirling at his encampment on the Gowanus and Port Roads,* arriving at about 3 o'clock in the morning. He ordered Stirling to collect as many troops as he could to stop Grant. Stirling immediately marched south with the two regiments he had on hand: 400 men (six companies) from Smallwood's Maryland Battalion, wearing their hunting shirts, and most of John Haslet's Delawares, in full regimental dress. Their colonels were in New York serving on a court-martial board and the units were commanded, respectively, by their majors, Mordecai Gist and Thomas McDonough. Stirling was soon followed by General Parsons with another 200 or so from Jedediah Huntington's Connecticut Continentals, and more from Samuel Atlee's Pennsylvanians.

At about 4:30 A.M., Putnam burst into Sullivan's tent near Battle Pass with the news that the major British offensive had begun on the Shore Road. Sullivan dispatched 400 of his command to help Stirling out. These arrived at about 9 A.M. Meanwhile, messengers had been sent to alert other commanders and signal lights on the telegraph on Brooklyn Heights sent word to Washington's headquarters in Manhattan.

To the east, however, Clinton, with his grenadiers and light infantry, was moving into position to roll up the American flank in his still-undetected drive toward the heart of the Continental Army's defenses.

By 8 A.M., Washington had arrived from New York. One enlisted man noted: "I saw him walk along the lines and give his orders in person to the colonels of each regiment. . . . I also heard Washington say, 'If I see any man turn his back today, I will shoot him through. I have two pistols loaded, but will not ask any man to go further than I do. I will fight as long as I have a leg or an arm.' . . . He said the time had come when Americans must be freemen or slaves. Quit yourselves like men (he told us), like soldiers, for all that is worth living for is at stake."[2]

Washington also called for reinforcements from New York. A

---

*This is the site of the Old Stone House where Stirling and the Marylanders made their stand later in the day. There is no conclusive evidence whether Stirling had or had not spent the night in the house.

fifteen-year-old private, Joseph Plum Martin,* who had joined the Connecticut levie in June for six months as he "wished only to take a priming
before I took upon me the whole coat of paint for a soldier,"[3] wrote:

> . . . as soon as the regiment was formed, we were marched off for
> the ferry. At the lower end of the street were placed several casks
> of sea-bread . . . the casks were unheaded and each man was
> allowed to take as many as he could, as he marched by. . . . I
> improved the opportunity thus offered me, as every good soldier
> should on all important occasions, to get as many of the biscuits
> as I possibly could. . . .
>
> We quickly embarked on board the boats. As each boat
> started, three cheers were given by those on board, which was
> returned by the numerous spectators who thronged the wharves.
> They all wished us good luck, apparently, although it was with
> the most of them, perhaps, nothing more than ceremony.
>
> We soon landed at Brooklyn upon the Island, marched up
> the ascent from the ferry to the plain. We now began to meet the
> wounded men, another sight I was unacquainted with, some with
> broken arms, some with broken legs, and some with broken
> heads. The sight of these a little daunted me, and made me think
> of home, but the sight and thought vanished together. We
> marched a short distance, when we halted. . . .
>
> While resting here, which was not more than twenty
> minutes or half an hour, the Americans and British were warmly
> engaged within sight of us. . . .
>
> The officers of the new levies wore cockades of different
> colors to distinguish them from the standing forces, as they were
> called. The field officers wore red, the captains white, and the
> subaltern officers green. While we were resting here, our lieuten-
> ant colonel and major (our colonel not being with us) took their
> cockades from their hats. Being asked the reason, the lieutenant
> colonel replied that he was willing to risk his life in the cause of
> his country, but he was unwilling to stand a particular mark for
> the enemy to fire at. He was a fine officer and a brave soldier.[4]

---

*In Onderdonk he is identified as James S. Martin, who published in 1830 *The
Adventures of a Revolutionary Soldier.* See Bibliography.

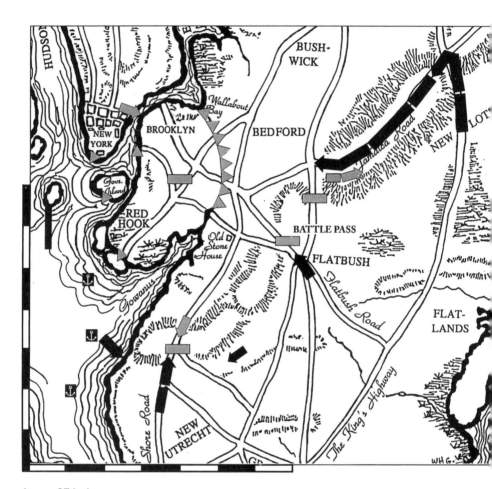

August 27th, 4 a.m.

14. "Lord Stirling's Last Struggle Around the Old Cortelyou House," by Alonzo
Chappel. The majority of the attacking Marylanders were killed in this
rearguard action that saved the remnants of the retreating American Army.

15. The departure of the Marylanders for New York, July 1776.

16. Left: Major Mordechai Gist, who commanded the Maryland regiment at Brooklyn. 17. Right: Israel Putnam, the legendary French and Indian War fighter, who also distinguished himself at Bunker Hill. Putnam's raw courage would avail him little against the British professionals at Brooklyn.

18. At Brooklyn, the British were able to land 6,000 men in their first wave, against negligible opposition.

19. Later in 1776, off Newport, Rhode Island, the British once again demonstrated their skill at amphibious movement. Throughout the war, their army would operate most successfully when in close proximity to their navy.

20. Above: In Brooklyn, American
soldiers chopped down trees to fo
roadblocks on the expected avenu
of British advance.
21. Below: Americans retreating
across Gowanus Creek—in reality,
there is little evidence they crosse
with flags flying.
22. Right: The evacuation of
Brooklyn begins.

23. Tavern owner William Howard was roused from bed by a party led by Generals Howe, Cornwallis, Clinton and Percy. After serving Howe a drink, he was forced by the British commander to show the British column the way to Gowanus.

24. Lord Stirling and the Marylanders in action at the height of the battle near the Old Stone House.

25. As Stirling and the Marylanders flung themselves against the converging British columns, the remnants of the forward American forces sought shelter across Gowanus Creek. A number of men drowned because the Americans had prematurely destroyed a bridge during the retreat. The structure at the right is Freeke's Mill.

26. Washington directs the evacuation which saved the army, and which would earn the admiration of British commanders for its near-flawless execution.

27. A European depiction of the British parade through New York on
September 19, 1776.

28. The Continental Army finally held its own New York victory parade in
1783, after seven long years of fighting.

*   *   *

"The solemn day had come at last, wrote the Reverend John Woodhull from Manhattan to his wife. "Long Island is made a field of blood — now the cannon and small arms make a continued roar. . . . Yea now it is roaring in my ears and God only knows when it will end."[5]

Day broke "with a Red and angry Glare"[6] wrote one officer in Clinton's corps. Now, through open country in the fields around the Jamaica Road, hard, traditional fighting might be expected as the heavy infantry, the Grenadiers, led the way westward. The way was open, the Jamaica Road was undefended and, as one American rifleman wrote afterward, reflecting some innocence, it was "a route we never dreamed of."[7]

By 8 A.M., as a result of hard night marching and poor American reconnaisance, the majority of Howe's force was in position *behind* the American advance lines. At other attack points, de Heister had his Hessians and Highlanders in position in front of Battle Pass; Grant had advanced along the Shore Road and was already in a heavy firefight at Martense Lane, but he did not commit his full force. Both waited for the signal from Clinton in the northeast.

Apart from some British cannonading, things had been relatively quiet for Sullivan at Battle Pass. Having detached 400 men to help Stirling at the Shore Road, where the main British thrust was expected, he now faced the imminent assault from de Heister with a force of not more than 800.

Near the Shore/Gowanus Roads, Atlee's Pennsylvanians had borne the brunt of the skirmishing with Grant's troops. At this time, 8 A.M., Stirling ordered Atlee to drop back so the British would have to face the fresh units he had now received. These new contingents were placed in open order across the road. Stirling's strongest unit, the Marylanders, were on his left, anchored in a hilltop copse of trees to take advantage of the only height available. There, they had waited since first light, about four hours, and had been the target of Grant's artillery.

Accompanying Howe's real main thrust was Captain Francis Rawdon, Lord Hastings, who later wrote: "[We]. . . marched with the greatest silence towards a pass some miles to the right of Flatbush, which being little known we thought would be but weakly guarded. . . . We got through the pass at daybreak without any opposition, and then turned to the left towards Bedford. When we were within a mile of that town, we heard firing. . . where General Grant was expected. We fired two pieces of cannon to let him know we were at hand."[8]

From the diary of Captain Archibald Robertson, Royal Engineers, also with Howe and Clinton: "When we came near to Bedford the Rebels began to fire from the Woods on our left which continued for some distance as we march'd on to Brooklyn."[9]

Colonel Samuel Miles had been ordered the previous day to keep an eye to the east, and stationed his unit — 600 Pennsylvanians and some New York troops — in the American front line near Bedford Pass. When he heard of the British breakthrough, he left behind Colonel Samuel Wylly's Continentals and other units, some 800 strong, to hold the pass, and started marching east. He passed, unknown, Clinton's advance units. Soon, though, the two forces met and exchanged fire. Miles had chanced on the tail end of the British column, the baggage train. He attacked it with his forward units and sent word to his second battalion, Lieutenant Colonel Broadhead commanding, to get back to Sullivan and alert him of this new danger. Clinton's men now had their first major chance at the enemy. Cut off and faced with overwhelming numbers, Miles' detachment could not stand against the British, and dispersed to fight their way to safety singly or in small groups. Half, including Miles, were captured at this point, while the rest, falling back along the Flatbush and Port Roads, made their way toward the inner lines at Brooklyn Neck.

Sullivan had heard the firing coming from his rear, heard Clinton's signal cannon, and was joined by Broadhead's battalion just as remnants of Miles' bloodied unit came straggling in. After previously dispatching reinforcements to the American right, Sullivan now realized the main British thrust had come up on the left and was now, in fact, behind him. Sullivan turned the greater part of his force to face the new threat, leaving the pass to be defended by his skirmishers and the artillery in a redoubt built earlier.

The British plan had worked. Diversions by Grant and de Heister had drawn the bulk of the American front-line forces to the west, leaving the way clear for an envelopment.

Assigning the light infantry and a detachment of cavalry to deal with Sullivan, Clinton led his column steadily along the Jamaica Road, roughly paralleling the route of today's Atlantic Avenue. Where it joined the Flatbush and Gowanus Roads, he turned south.

In the center, de Heister attacked along the Flatbush Road, while the Jaegers, in loose order, made their way as flankers through the heavy underbrush. His main column of Hessians, with the Highlanders of the 42nd, the Black Watch,* advanced along what was then a narrow track walled in by heavy foliage. A tree named after Provincial Governor Dongan, a large white oak standing just below Battle Pass — which served as a boundary marker between the townships of Brooklyn and Flatbush — had been cut down as a roadblock. It had been covered by fire from the American rifles on the hills above the pass and the cannon in the earthwork redoubt on the slope to the east.

Here, de Heister began the day with artillery fire on the redoubt to hold the Americans' attention while waiting for the signal from Clinton. When he heard the cannon fire from the north, de Heister ordered Colonel von Donop forward.

Somewhat unusual for the place, along a rough, meandering path through a dense forest de Heister had placed two ranks of young drummers and fifers in the van, taking the point of the column. Then came companies of the line with bayonets fixed. The Americans had depended on the deadly fire of their long rifles, but the thick foliage masking the twisting road that covered the advancing enemy made their extreme range and accuracy useless.

On de Heister's flanks, the Jaegers, carrying only haversacks, made their way through the underbrush, taking cover behind trees and rocks and firing with their short forest rifles as targets appeared.

---

*So named, in Scots Gaelic, *Freicgdan Dubh.* From the dark colors of its tartan, as distinguished from the regular troops: *Saighdean Dearg,* or "red soldiers." The unit had seen much service in the New World: at Ticonderoga, or Fort Carillon as the French called it, and at Quebec — two of the three "Gibraltars of America," the third being Louisbourg. These soldiers were recruited from the west of Scotland and spoke Scots Gaelic as their mother tongue. Their appearance, as well as the skirl of the bagpipe which accompanied them into battle, could unnerve an inexperienced foe, particularly when they unleashed their battle cry.

The Hessians, from field-grade officer down, fought on foot. Horses had only been brought from the Germanies for senior officers and none had been provided as yet for the intermediate grades. One Hessian subaltern wrote: "Almost all the officers of the staff and the subaltern officers were on foot, their cloaks rolled up on their shoulders and a large canteen, filled with rum and water, suspended from their sides. I had to do the same, although I acted as an aid (*sic*); and whenever my brigade general, Col. von Donop, wished to send a dispatch, he alighted and gave me his old but good steed, which he had brought over from Hessia."[10]

The commanding and staff officers also carried carbines — short, rifled guns. Von Donop used his to shoot one American through the head who had been aiming his rifle at him. Those officers in the fighting line carried the smooth-bore musket with bayonet. Partly due to the heat of the day and partly because of the irregular country, the foot soldiers were allowed to sling their short sabers across their breasts. This permitted them to wear their heavy wool regimental coats unbuttoned and kept the swords from getting entangled in the thick foliage.

With Howe's forces at Battle Pass now converging, British forward units fell on Sullivan's new front. The Highlanders and Hessians, meanwhile, finally unleashed after long months of anticipation, forced the pass with a single bayonet charge.

Said Archibald Robertson: "About 9 o'clock the Rebels gave way very fast and in their retreat, across marsh and mill dam, received heavy fire from our Grenadiers tho' distant. The Light Horse could not act for a swamp that was in front. At the same time General Clinton was sent from Flatlands, General Grant March'd from Dinnys' (*sic*) with 2 Brigades to turn the Rebels right flank and Count Dunhop (*sic*) march'd in Centre from Flat Bush. . ."[11]

Hessian Major Baurmeister later wrote to a friend: "We soon saw them come through the woods to attack us. We routed them the first onset, and pursued them so close through the thickest woods that they never could rally. . . . The [British] Light Infantry who were first engaged dashed in as fast as foot could carry. The scoundrels were driven into the wood and out of the wood, where they had supposed that we should never venture to engage them."[12]

Admiral Howe's secretary, Ambrose Serle, would report: "From what I saw myself nothing could exceed [our] Spirit and Intrepidity in attacking the Enemy. In one thing only they failed — they could not run so fast as their Foes, many of whom indeed [were] ready to run over each other."[13]

Stephen Kemble, with Clinton's column, summarized the action of the next few hours: "About a mile before we came to Bedford we saw the Rebels on our Left. The Light Infantry [were] ordered to attack them which they did with success and drove them every way; the Grenadiers continued the road to Brooklyn with the general at their head to cut off the Enemy's Retreat from Brookland Heights which was happily executed. [In the center] Lieut.-Gen. de Heister attacked from Flatbush at the same time & [on the British left] Major-Gen. Grant with the Fourth & Sixth Brigade from the Heights of the Narrows [moving up from Fort Hamilton] by which measure the Rebels were cut off from all Retreat and cooped up in the woods to the Right of the road from Brooklyn to Flatlands. Major-Gen. Grant had attacked early in the morning, but the Enemy under Brigadier-General Lord Stirling & Major-Gen. Sullivan being strongly posted in the woods could not proceed far. The action between them and part of the Main body continued until late in the afternoon."[14] Thus, with Grant and de Heister pressing from the south and Clinton sealing off retreat on the east and north, the American outer defenses were surrounded.

A German historian, Max von Elking, writing well after the event, described the part the Hessians took at Battle Pass:

As soon as Gen. von (*sic*) Heister heard the reports of artillery on his right and knew, from its direction, that the flanking movement had succeeded, he formed quickly for the attack. In front were the grenadiers, in three divisions, and in front of them, as flankers, a company of yagers (*sic*) under Capt. Wredon. The brigade von Mirbach covered the left flank. The troops advanced bravely, with martial music sounding and colors flying, and ascended the hills in the best order — the men dragging the cannons with the greatest caution through the dense forest. When, with but little loss by the enemy's artillery, the troops had reached the crest of the hill, the line was formed with as much care as on the parade-ground. The Americans [rifle skirmishers] were quickly driven back by the advancing flankers—many were killed or captured—while the Hessian regiments followed with closed ranks and shouldered muskets. "The enemy," wrote Col. von Heeringen to Col. von Lossberg, "had almost impenetrable thickets, lines, abatis, and redoubts before him. The riflemen were mostly pierced by the bayonets to the trees. These terrible men deserve more pity than fear—they want nearly fifteen minutes for loading their pieces, and during that time they feel our balls and bayonets! The yagers of the left wing, eager for the combat, rushed forward so rapidly that their captain could not restrain them. They penetrated the works of the American encampment, and saw it on their left, a redoubt to their right. The Americans, surprised by the sudden appearance of the Hessians, rallied into groups of fifty to sixty men; but having no time to form, were shot down, dispersed, or captured. This happened in view of the garrison within the enemy's lines."

The Americans supposed that the Hessians would not give quarter. Every one of them tried to sell his life as dearly as possible, or to save it by flight, while the Hessians grew more exasperated and angry in consequence of this apparently obstinate and useless resistance. Therefore ensued a violent contest, here in larger or smaller crowds, there in wild and irregular rout. A part tried to escape into the woods, but a great many fell into the swamps and perished miserably, or were captured. Only a small number succeeded in cutting their way through and reaching their lines. The Hessians fired only once [a volley], and then attacked with their bayonets.[15]

Up the Flatbush Road, de Heister's Hessians and Highlanders poured onto the 400 Massachusetts troops Sullivan had left to hold the pass. From both sides, the enemy came yelling and stabbing with their bayonets; the Americans used their rifles as best as they could, as clubs. Surrounded and greatly outnumbered, the surviving defenders of Battle Pass surrendered.* Their damask flag bearing the word "Liberty" fell to the enemy.

The 60 Americans who surrendered with the flag to the Hessians were lucky. Others, not so. All over the field, many who tried to surrender were slaughtered and stragglers were shot down or bayoneted when they could not escape. Hessians with leveled bayonets formed circles around terrified groups of Americans in the woods; methodically these rings would close until all life within them was extinguished.

Though the Hessians and Highlanders accounted for much of this massacre, the British troops from Clinton's column did more than their share of the killing, falling like a torrent on the 400 men Sullivan had taken toward Bedford. When these met Clinton's advance forces, and saw that they faced overwhelming odds, the men of Sullivan's detachment made a somewhat orderly retreat. But on the western slope of Mount Prospect, where the Central Branch of the Brooklyn Public Library now stands, they were fallen upon by Light Infantry and Dragoons and hurled back on the bayonets of the advancing Hessians. It was now high noon.

A British officer with Fraser's Highland battalion wrote: "Rejoice . . . that we have given the Rebels a d----d crush. . . . The Hessians and our brave Highlanders gave no quarter, and it was a fine sight to see with what alacrity they dispatched the Rebels with their bayonets after we had surrounded them so that they could not resist. . . . It was a glorious achievement . . . and will immortalize us and crush the rebel colonies. Our loss was nothing. We took care to tell the Hessians that the rebels had resolved to give no quarter — to them in particular — which made them fight desperately, and put all to death that fell into their hands."[16] Earlier, the British had made a point to spread the rumor in the Hessian ranks that the Americans indeed practiced cannibalism on defeated enemies, noting, as evidence, the tomahawk each man carried.

A British field-grade officer who seemed to have a greater claim to humanity than the one cited just above, and who certainly showed his chivalrous and compassionate nature, commented: "The Americans fought bravely and (to do them justice) could not be broken till greatly outnumbered and taken flank, front and rear. We were greatly shocked

---

*On the spot of the engagement, Battle Pass in Prospect Park, is a boulder that once bore a bronze plaque: "Line of Defense / Aug. 27, 1776 / Battle of Long Island / 175 Feet South / Site of Valley Grove House / 150 Feet North."

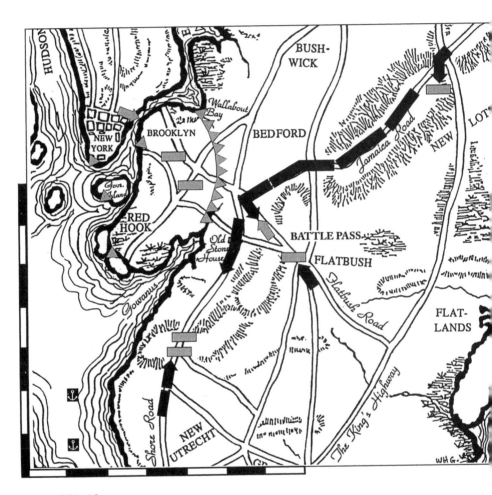

August 27th, 10 a.m.

by the massacres made by the Hessians and Highlanders after victory was decided."[17]

In defense of the Hessian actions, Max von Elking noted: "Great excitement and rage on the part of the Hessians cannot be denied, but it was chiefly caused by some squads of the enemy, who, after being surrounded and having asked for quarter, fired again upon the unsuspecting Hessians, who had advanced towards them [to accept their surrender]." The British surpassed the Hessians in that respect. Von Elking, quoting from a letter from von Heeringen, reveals, " 'The English did not give much quarter. . . and continually incited our troops to do the same.' We have seen in his letter, as previously quoted, how treacherously Col. John acted towards the Hessian grenadier, and how the Pennsylvania regiment, after having been surrounded, gave another volley. The natural consequence of this was an increase of the fury of well-disciplined troops, unused to such a manner of fighting. That the Hessians did not massacre all their enemies, we have seen from the fact that the regiment Rall, encountering a squad of Americans, made them prisoners without cruelty."[18]

In his diary, a German Lieutenant Ruffer recorded his impression that the Americans were loath to surrender: "They were so much frightened that they preferred being shot down to taking quarter, because their generals and officers had told them that they would be hanged."[19]

But some did surrender and some made a separate peace with the enemy. Von Elking wrote: "Amongst the prisoners are many, so-called, colonels, lieut.-colonels, and majors, and other officers, who have all previously been tailors, shoemakers, barbers, etc. Some of them have been badly beaten by our men, because the latter did not consider them real officers. I did not find among the captured officers a single one who had been in foreign service before. They are all rebels and settled citizens. My Lord Stirling is nothing but an *échappé de famille.* He resembles my Lord Granby as one egg the other.* General Putnam is a

---

*John Manners, Marquis of Granby (1721–70), was one of the most aggressive and victorious British cavalry generals in Germany during the Seven Years' War. In addition to his military prowess, Granby was noted for his warm disposition and the pleasure he took from drinking while off duty. His portrait, with reddened nose and cheeks, adorns the signs of the many public houses in England named after him.

butcher by profession. The rebels desert frequently. It is not uncommon to see colonels, lieutenant-colonels, and majors coming into our lines with a number of men. The captured colors, made of red damask, with the motto 'Liberty,' came with sixty men to the regiment Rall; they carried their muskets upside down, their hats under their arms, fell upon their knees, and begged for quarter."[20]

The captive Americans were put to work dragging cannon and moving stores over the almost impassable roads. This enforced labor seems to have been due less to insolence on the part of the victors than to the exigencies of battle: to move equipment quickly and save the strength of the British troops, almost at the point of exhaustion at this time, for any further fighting.

The American Revolution was the second war of national liberation the British had fought, the first being the Jacobite "Rising of the Forty-Five," only a generation earlier. On April 16, 1746, some 5,000 Scots Highlanders were routed by 12,000 British regulars under William, Duke of Cumberland, who earned the title "The Butcher" after the massacre of the Scottish wounded and those who had surrendered. Perhaps the British thought the rules differed in the case of wars such as the American Revolution and the Scottish rising from those of more traditional fighting for territorial and commercial advantage.

At the same time, the rules of warfare in the 18th century, when applied, depended on the word of officers. An offer to give quarter, or surrender, was the word of a gentleman and no treachery was expected. The sham surrenders by some groups of Americans so enraged the officers and men on the British side that, as a reaction, all rules of conduct would naturally have been suspended.

As the bloodletting ended at Battle Pass, some Hessian units, principally Jaegers, began moving along the Port Road leading down to the Gowanus, pressing against the retreating Americans. Those from Sullivan's command who were able were now dragging the wounded down this relatively straight, narrow road, hedged in by thick foliage. When the Germans got to the top of the slope with a clear field of fire, they opened up with their carbines. Soon, some Hessians dragged up an American cannon they had just found abandoned, and commenced firing at the retreating troops.

CHAPTER X

"Our men fought with more than Roman valor"

IN BROOKLYN, George Washington could only be a spectator at what seemed to be the impending destruction of his army. The wounded and stragglers making their way back to the inner lines brought news of one disaster after another. Although some told of individual acts of heroism against superior forces, others brought news of desertion and cowardice in the face of the enemy; still others reported on the massacre of their comrades who had surrendered.

In the early morning the only hopeful sign was on the Shore/ Gowanus Roads, where the American troops seemed to be holding firm against Grant. By mid-morning, however, from his position atop the fort on the 90-foot-high Ponkiesberg, Washington could see Howe's strategy played out. Soon this, the last of the American contingents still intact on the field, would be surrounded and crushed by a twenty-to-one British advantage in manpower.

On this right flank, a cross section of the American Army, from the most inept militia units to the best Washington had, troops from Connecticut, New York, Pennsylvania, Delaware and Maryland, under Generals Stirling and Parsons, had held out since well before dawn. And on this right flank, for Stirling and the Maryland Brigade—who were to earn with their blood the title "Immortals"—the finest moment was yet to come.

The British left wing began its push early in the morning, where the southernmost part of the Green-Wood Cemetery is today, and continued to Martense Lane and the Gowanus Road at the Red Lion Inn. This position was defended by the 2nd New York, as well as by the Pennsylvania Militias commanded by Colonels Hand and Atlee — a total of about 600 men. Stirling arrived before dawn with the Maryland and Delaware contingents; Parsons shortly brought up the troops he had collected on his way south. And when the 400 men Sullivan had detached from Battle Pass arrived, this would bring the American force at this point to over 2,000.

Facing the Americans were the 4th and 6th Brigades, 42nd Regiment and two companies of loyalist New York Provincials raised by Governor Tryon in the spring.

After the skirmishing escalated at the watermelon patch, Grant began applying pressure before dawn with heavy cannon fire. Shortly before sunrise, the British ran low on shot and powder and Grant signaled his needs to Admiral Howe. The munitions were brought from the storeships and carried up the hill to the lines by a steady procession of sailors. The Admiral, however, to ensure a stronger navy presence, landed 2,000 Royal Marines at Bennet's Cove (at the southern tip of Gowanus Bay) between 10 and 11 A.M. to reinforce Grant. This allowed almost all the marines available to share in the glory of what looked to be an imminent British victory, and they brought Grant's manpower to about 9,000.

While Grant was waiting for resupply, the American forward units under Hand and Atlee fell back a few hundred yards through the line of Maryland troops Stirling had placed across the road. Here they rested, occupying a more fortified position, Blockje's Berg, or Barracks, a small steep hill near Sylvan Lake in Green-Wood. Shortly, Stirling's line also retired to the hill to consolidate forces. The Americans were joined by Sullivan's detachment at about 9 A.M., and held out under ever-increasing pressure as Grant applied still more troops to the engagement.

Stirling formed his line with Atlee's troops on his right, nearest the coast, at about today's 18th Street, under cover of trees to act in ambush as skirmishers. On Blockje's hill, between 18th and 20th Streets, to the east of the Gowanus Road, was Stirling's main formation, and two companies were placed just in front to buffer an English charge. Just in front to the left, at what would be about 23rd Street, was a detachment of the Maryland Regiment.

On the map they formed an inverted "V" or, as an invention of Frederick the Great of Prussia, a "kettle" (*kessel* in German), with the legs of the "V" ready to envelop any British units attacking Stirling's main force at the juncture of the two arms. In addition to occupying the higher ground, the Americans had the further advantage of a small stream in front of them crossed only by a narrow bridge on the Gowanus Road.

"The British then advanced within about 300 yards of us," wrote an American rifleman, "and began a very heavy fire from their cannon and mortars: for both the balls and shells flew very fast, now and then taking off a head. Our men stood it amazingly well, not even one showed a disposition to shrink. Our orders were not to fire till the enemy came within 50 yards of us; but when they perceived we stood their fire so cooly (*sic*) and resolutely, they declined coming any nearer, though treble our number. In this situation we stood from sunrise till 12 o'clock, the enemy firing on us the chief part of the time."[1]

Stirling was saving his first volley until it could take the greatest effect—at close distance—and just before the bayonet charge, or a withdrawal. Often in the 18th-century smooth-bore battles, as the lines slowly approached, opposing commanders would goad each other to fire first, giving the side with their muskets still loaded the advantage. Stirling had his troops in a loose, open order of two ranks while Grant's larger force was packed closely together in three ranks, providing a more productive target for any volley by Stirling. (In many 18th-century battles casualties in volley fire were heavier in proportion on the side with the greater number of troops engaged.)

Recalling Howe's orders, Lord Percy noted: "The Troops should receive the Rebels' first fire and then rush on them before they had recovered their arms, with their bayonets, which threw them [the Americans met by Clinton's division, possibly Sullivan's command] into the utmost confusion they being unacquainted with such a maneuver."[2]

"About this time the enemy began to send detachments as scouts on our left," wrote Second Lieutenant William Popham of Haslet's

Delawares, "when Capt. Wragg [of the Royal Marines] and 18 men, supposing us to be Hessians by the similarity of our dress, approached too near before he discovered his mistake, when my company attacked and took them prisoners."[3] A British officer wrote: "The 2nd battalion of grenadiers, which was sent from our right to support Gen. Grant, unfortunately mistook a rebel regiment [blue faced with red] for the Hessians, and received several fires from them without returning it; and Lt. Wragg of the marines, and 20 men, being sent out to speak to them, were made prisoner. . . ."[4] Popham continued:

> I was immediately ordered with a guard to convey them across the creek in our rear to our lines. On descending the high ground we reached a salt meadow, over which we passed, though not miry, yet very unfavorable to silk stockings and my over-clothes. When we had reached about half way to the creek, the enemy brought a couple of pieces to bear upon us, which, when Wragg saw, he halted in the hope of a rescue; but on my ordering him to march forward instantly, or I should fire on him, he moved on. When we got to the creek, the bank of which was exceedingly muddy, we waded up to our waists. I got in after my people and prisoners, and an old canoe that had been split and [made] incapable of floating except by the buoyancy of the wood, served to help those who wanted help to cross a deep hole in the creek, by pushing it across from the bank which it had reached. I had advanced so far into the mud, and was so fatigued with anxiety and exercise, that I sat down on the mud with the water up to my breast, Wragg's fusee [flintlock rifle], cartouche box, and bayonet on my shoulder; in which situation I sat till my charge were all safely landed on the rear.[5]

Although Popham's arrival in the rear with prisoners in tow was no doubt impressive to the men in the entrenchments on Brooklyn Neck, the fact is that by 10:00 A.M., there was nothing remaining of the American advance lines in the east. All cohesion there had by now been broken and the men remaining in the field were either dead, captives of the British or fugitives hiding in the brush and hills. The Hessians and Highlanders had smashed through the American center, at Battle Pass in Flatbush, and Cornwallis, with the bulk of the British forces, had continued from Jamaica Pass, dispersing the American left to come up on their remaining right wing from behind.

The American right—men from Maryland, Delaware, Connecticut, New York and Pennsylvania, under Stirling's command—was still standing firm against Grant's regulars around the Shore Road. But with all three British columns now converging, the climax of the battle was at hand.

*   *   *

As the encounter evolved on the Shore/Gowanus Roads, it proved to be the most heroic action of the day. Before the battle, Stirling repeated to his troops Grant's boast that he could march across the colonies with 5,000 British regulars, and said: "We are not so many, but I think we are enough to prevent his advancing farther over the Continent than this millpond."[6]

As the morning wore on, Stirling's command—once 2,000 men—diminished in numbers through casualties taken; the British were constantly being reinforced. From the south, Grant grew in strength: he was reinforced early in the morning by 2,000 of the 42nd Highlanders sent him by de Heister, and later by the 2,000 Royal Marines from Admiral Howe. From the north, Hessians poured through Battle Pass, coming down the Port Road to join Cornwallis' column attacking Stirling's rear. Cornwallis, with part of Fraser's Highlanders—the 71st Regiment—and the Second Grenadiers, plus his growing contingent of Hessians, seized the thick-walled fieldstone-and-brick Vechte-Cortelyou house* standing near today's 5th Avenue and 3rd Street, a major strong point.

When Stirling learned of Cornwallis' presence to his rear, he took the Marylanders—Major Gist and a reinforced heavy company, nearly 400 men—and rushed north along the Gowanus Road, leaving the bulk of his forces under General Parsons to hold off Grant while executing as orderly a retreat as possible to the inner lines. The British pressure on

---

*A natural fortification built in 1699 to withstand Indian raids. It is also known as the Old Stone House at Gowanus.

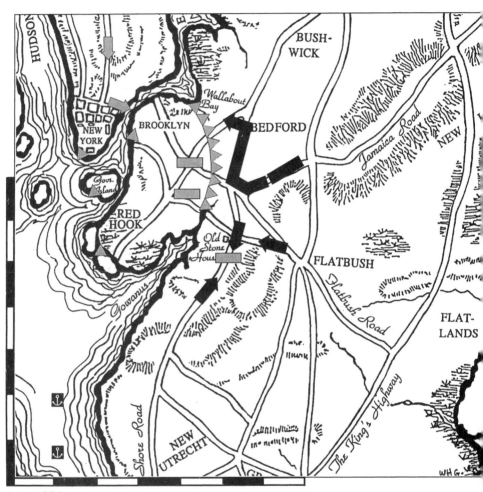

August 27th, noon

the right, however, simply became too great. Even Atlee's Pennsylvanians finally broke. With Cornwallis, reinforced by the Hessians and Highlanders, coming up in the rear, rallying by the stone house that commanded the American escape route, the entire American right wing was threatened with annihilation.

Although having sustained fire throughout the morning, Gist's Marylanders were relatively fresh. With their training, discipline, muskets and bayonets they just might be able to hold Cornwallis. Though they were barely 400 men, massed in front of them was a British force of 2,000 — and growing. Cornwallis brought up a light cannon and placed it in the Old Stone House, soon to be joined by several heavier guns, sited around the position. Behind him, Stirling could see individuals and units of his command now desperately trying to get back across the Gowanus Creek to the inner American lines.

There was only one way for Stirling to stop the inexorable British tide, and that was to attack. Into a rain of British fire the Marylanders charged, and Cornwallis recoiled, stunned by the unexpected rebel onslaught. Though the ground became littered with dead and dying Maryland militia, Stirling formed them up again. Again, they attacked, closing up the line when comrades fell, reforming and attacking again, their numbers diminishing by the minute. Six times Stirling charged, and twice the assaults drove the British from the stone house.

Each attack was met with withering counterfire as the British masses swelled against this fanatically determined American rearguard. As Stirling launched his last assault, with a remaining handful of men, even more British reinforcements arrived. At last, the remnant of the Marylanders broke into small parties to fight their way to safety. In the last attack Stirling himself was captured by some Hessians who had outrun their unit. But he refused to give up to Cornwallis, the senior British commander on the scene. Instead, on searching out de Heister, he surrendered his sword to the Hessian commander. Cornwallis later said, "General Lord Stirling fought like a wolf."[7]

Stirling's and the Marylanders' gallant action allowed the rest of the Americans remaining in the field to escape across the Gowanus Creek and survive. Only seven men crossing the Gowanus were lost through drowning. But the Marylanders had sacrificed themselves for the sake

of the army. Out of barely 400 men, 256 lay dead in front of the Old
Stone House. Over a hundred others were wounded and/or captured.
Only Gist and nine others managed to regain the American lines.

This sacrifice was to be remembered throughout the war. According
to someone unidentified in any history book: "The Declaration of
Independence that was signed in ink in Philadelphia was signed in blood
in south Brooklyn."*

* * *

A smaller action took place on a hill a mile south of the Old Stone House
where an unidentified, company-sized unit of American riflemen had
taken position. The hill rises steeply above the Gowanus Road at about
present-day 24th Street. There, because of their commanding position
and the sparce foliage, the Americans, for the first time in the battle,
were able to make use of the accuracy of their long rifles. They concentrated their fire on officers of units from Cornwallis' column that had
bypassed the Old Stone House to clean out pockets of resistance. Garret
Bergen, who was a boy at that time, recalled one British officer who
dashed into his family's farmhouse, dropped into a chair and said of the
determined American rifle fire that "he'd be d----d if he was going to
expose himself to that fire, that the d----d rascals picked out all the
officers."[8]

Some of the Americans had posted themselves in trees to get a
better field of fire. One, who killed Lieutenant Colonel James Grant and
another officer, was discovered and a British squad fired a volley into the
tree, dispatching him. The two British officers were buried in a field,
but the American sniper's body was left to rot on the ground as an

---

*On the Altar to Liberty on the Battle Path in the Green-Wood Cemetery, is inscribed
the "first prize poem" by Sarah I. Day, written in 1913: "Here and along the slopes of
Greenwood's hills/our patriots for the first time faced their foe/in open field; And well
we stood the test./'Men!' cried Lord Stirling, as we formed our line,/'This Grant who
comes against us once declared/in England's House of Commons—I sat there/and
heard—that given him five thousand men/he'd cross our continent from end to
end!/He has his number now, I doubt not we/A fourth as many, yet I promise you/
He'll march no farther through our continent/than Brower's mill ponds yonder.'" In
one of history's ironies, Grant ended his military career as governor of Stirling Castle in
Scotland.

example. Civilians were prohibited from burying it. A few days later, though, a storm felled the tree and late the next night his body was placed in the cavity left by the roots and covered with earth.

This American position on the hill was soon surrounded and rushed, and the defenders shot. The fallen were buried where they lay. It is now Battle Hill in Green-Wood Cemetery, where the Altar to Liberty stands.

An American rifleman who had faced Grant's skirmishers earlier wrote:

> ...and the main body of British...had surrounded us, and driven within the lines or scattered in the woods, all our men except the Delaware and Maryland battalions, who were standing at the bay with double their number. Thus situated, we were ordered to attempt a retreat by fighting our way through the enemy, who had posted themselves and nearly filled every road and field between us and our lines. We had not retreated a quarter of a mile, before we were fired on by an advanced party of the enemy, and those in the rear playing their artillery on us. Our men fought with more than Roman valor. We forced the advanced party which first attacked us to give way, through which opening we got a passage down to the side of a marsh, seldom before waded over, which we passed, and then swam a narrow river, all the while exposed to the enemy's fire. . . . The whole of the right wing of our battalion, thinking it impossible to march through the marsh, attempted to force their way through the woods, where they, almost to a man, were killed or taken...[9]

Colonel William Smallwood had been delayed on a court-martial board in New York and only reached Brooklyn in time to watch his Marylanders at the Old Stone House. He described what he saw from the inner fortifications near Freeke's tidal-mill dam, a bridge on the Port Road over the Gowanus Creek: "Between the place of action and our lines there lay a large marsh and deep creek, not above 80 yards across at the mouth, (the place of action upon a direct line did not much exceed a mile from a part of our lines,) towards the head of which creek there was a *mill and bridge,* across which a certain Col. Ward, from New

England [21st Massachusetts Continentals], who is charged with having acted a bashful part that day, passed over with his regiment and then burnt them down, though under cover of our cannon, which would have checked the enemy's pursuit at any time, otherwise this bridge might have afforded a secure retreat. There then remained no other prospect but to surrender or attempt to retreat over this marsh and creek at the mouth, where no person had ever been known to cross. In the interim I applied to Gen. Washington for some regiments to march out to support and cover their retreat, which he urged would be attended with too great risk to the party and the lines."[10] Washington did order two guns drawn up opposite the brigade to support the endangered men.

The Connecticut unit of fifteen-year-old Private Martin, quoted earlier, along with one 12-pound cannon, had been ordered to cover Stirling. Said the boy: "We were soon called upon to fall in and proceed. . . . Our officers. . . pressed forward towards a creek, where a large party of Americans and British were engaged. By the time we arrived, the enemy had driven our men into the creek, or rather mill-pond (the tide being up), where such as could swim got across; those that could not swim and could not procure anything to buoy them up, sunk. The British having several field pieces stationed by a brick house* were pouring canister and grape upon the Americans like a shower of hail; they would doubtless have done them much more damage than they did but for the twelve-pounder. . . . The men having got it within sufficient distance to reach them, and opening a fire upon them, soon obliged them to shift their quarters."[11]

A chaplain, Philip Vickers Fithvan, also watched the action and described the events from early morning to the end: "They [Stirling's men] stood firm in a large body, on a good eminence in our plain view, but where we could give them no relief! On three sides of them were the enemy, on the other side was a broad marsh or creek. There the brave men stood for more than four hours [since dawn]. They found their enemies surrounding them more. At last they divided; placed a body to attack the enemy while a good part crossed over the water. Here was a desperate fire. But it was the best they could do. The officers swam

*The Old Stone House had brick gable ends that faced the American lines.

their horses over; the men some swam and some passed in boats, but many stood behind, among them Lord Stirling."[12]

Private Martin continued: "There was in this action a regiment of Maryland troops (volunteers), all young gentlemen. When they came out of the water and mud to us, looking like water rats, it was a truly pitiful sight. Many of them were killed in the pond and more were drowned. Some of us went into the water after the fall of the tide, and took a number of corpses and a great many arms that were sunk in the pond and creek."[13]

Washington, along with Putnam and some other generals, was watching from an observation post on Cobble Hill. An American rifleman later wrote: "Most of our generals on a high hill in the lines, viewed us with glasses, as we were retreating, and saw the enemy we had to pass through, thought we could not. Many thought we would surrender in a body without firing. When we began the attack, General Washington wrung his hands and cried out, 'Good God! what brave fellows I must this day lose!' "[14]

The Marylanders were buried in their uniforms of scarlet and buff where the one-acre farm of Adrian Van Brunt rose above the swamp near today's Third Avenue, between Seventh and Eighth Streets. Until the widening of the avenue in 1910, the burial site was memorialized by a tablet that read: "Burial place of ye 256 Maryland soldiers who fell in ye combat at ye Cortelyou House on ye 27th day of August 1776." Their heroism prevented the abject defeat of the Continental Army at the beginning of the war.

The day had, in fact, been won by the British, but once the smoke of battle subsided, an objective viewer, had there been one, might have summarized the events of the preceding few hours as far less than a strategic victory. Howe had successfully landed his army intact, turned the enemy's flank, inflicted heavy casualties, taken a considerable number of prisoners and captured five guns and at least two standards. While maintaining the integrity of his forces, he had demolished the entire outer defenses of the enemy. But he had not destroyed his opponent, and he had not taken the Americans' major defensive positions.

In short, despite the fact that he had some 30,000 effective troops to hand, Howe had neither shaken the rebels' political resolve nor destroyed their military effectiveness. Such a cool review more than two hundred years after the battle might, however, have come as a great surprise to any of the desperately tired and demoralized troops huddled inside the American entrenchments at the time.

CHAPTER XI

"How many were lost upon the Island is yet uncertain"

T RUE TO THE PRINCIPLES of continental warfare, Howe had outmaneuvered Washington and won the battle. Apart from British
mopping-up operations, organized mass combat was over around noon.
A thousand Americans were lying dead and waiting to be buried.
Scattered parties of the living were still hiding in the forests and swamps
or trying to make their way to their inner lines around Brooklyn Heights.
But in all sectors even the skirmishing was over by mid-afternoon. Many
had surrendered. Sullivan, who had commanded the American center,
was a prisoner; Stirling had also been taken captive.

British Captain Archibald Robertson wrote: "A Battalion of our
Grenadiers and the 71st were sent on towards General Grant and about
2 in the Afternoon they had a very smart Skirmish in the woods with the
Rebels who were trying to get to the water side to escape. The Hessians
likewise fell in with the flying Partys and they were drove from every
Quarter. We lost some Good Officers, about 60 men kill'd and about
300 wounded, the Rebel loss was very considerable upward of 3000,
wounded and Prisoners. Amongst the latter General Sullivan and Lord
Stirling. They had about 12,000 men on the heights. Great numbers got
across the creek into the works on Brooklyn heights, we were in
Possession of very good Ground within 600 Yards of them, and by some
mistake in orders had very near evacuated the ground. In the evening
we retired a little. The whole of this days Manoeuvre was well plann'd

and Executed, only more of the Rebels might have been cut off had we push'd on from Brooklyn sooner towards General Grant."[1]

The Hessian colonel von Heeringen recorded: "It looked horrible in the wood, as at least two thousand killed and wounded lay there."[2]

Howe estimated that the Americans lost thirty-three hundred men, 1,097 of them taken prisoner. Colonel Kemble estimated: "The rebels lost upward of 3,000 men, 3 General Officers — Major-Gen. Sullivan, Brigadier-Gen. Lord Stirling and Brigadier-Gen. Woodhull,* three colonels, 4 lieut.-colonels, 3 majors, 18 captains and upward of 1,100 men taken Prisoners, most of them Riflemen of whom they lost 1500."[3] The British dead and wounded numbered 373.

American estimates showed almost a reversal of figures. Reverend John Woodhull wrote to his wife Sally from Manhattan on August 30th: "How many men were lost upon the Island is yet uncertain, some say we have 700 missing and that we have killed twice as many of the enemy, tho I believe it is guesswork as yet."[4]

"General Sullivan I believe is taken prisoner," wrote one American soldier. "The last I heard of him, he was in a corn field close by our lines with a pistol in each hand, and the enemy had formed a line each side of him, and he was going directly between them. I like to have been taken prisoner myself; crossing from the lower road to the Bedford, I came close upon the advanced party of the enemy. I very luckily got within the lines time enough to give the alarm or I believe they would have been in upon us in surprise, for we had not at that time above two thousand men in our lines."[5]

Lists of American losses are incomplete. Of the 70 units under Washington the returns from 52 are unlocated. Of the others, some list names of wounded, killed, prisoner or missing, some give only raw numbers and the remainder were either not compiled or were lost to history. It seems the greatest casualty figures were on the Shore / Gowanus Roads.

---

*General Nathaniel Woodhull (1722–76), who was not part of the Brooklyn action, was captured in Jamaica by a reconnaissance party. Saying "God save us all" instead of "God save the King" as his captors ordered, he was struck on the head by a cutlass and his arm was run through by a bayonet. While in captivity he died of his wounds in September despite the efforts of his wife, who tended to him daily.

As best as can be reconstructed, losses included: Huntington's 7th Continentals (Connecticut), 199; Smallwood's Maryland Regiment, 267 (including 11 killed earlier); Atlee's Pennsylvania Musketeers, 89; Katchlein's Pennsylvania Militia, 27; Haslet's Delaware Battalion, 261; plus an unidentified company on Battle Hill ranging from 50 to 100 men, who were wiped out. Trapped at Bedford was Miles' Pennsylvania Rifle Regiment, which lost 209 killed or missing. Wylly's command at Bedford Pass, some 800 strong, disintegrated in the melee, some gaining safety, some not. The returns from the massacre at Battle Pass are nonexistent, but estimates have ranged to near 500. A culling of diaries, accounts and letters lists the names of fifteen lost in Sullivan's field command. Additional losses mentioned by name come to 53, bringing the total to a confirmed 1,120 — not counting the estimates from Battle and Bedford Passes, Bedford Village and Battle Hill.

Howe gave 349 as the British Army losses: 61 killed, 257 wounded and 31 missing. This does not include the capture of Captain Wragg and his 20 Royal Marines, who would be listed as losses by the Royal Navy. Two Hessian privates were killed and three of their officers and 23 men were wounded. Sorting through conflicting reports of losses, historian Henry R. Stiles, in the 1860s, suggested the British figures to be the most accurate: "Our own examination of the matter inclines us to accept the British and Hessian estimate as being most nearly correct. As *masters of the field,* they had the best opportunity of knowing the facts, nor can we see that they have been guilty of much exaggeration."[6]

Though the day ended with great suffering and loss, the exploits of those in the battle, particularly the Marylanders, served to strengthen the resolve of those Americans who had not actually been in, or close to, the fighting. Writing to her husband, John, on September 9th, Abigail Adams noted: "We have had many stories concerning engagements upon Long Island this week, of our lines being forced and of our troops returning to New York. . . . All we can learn is that we have been unsuccessful there, having many men as prisoners, among whom are Lord Stirling and General Sullivan. But if we should be defeated, I think we shall not be conquered. A people fired, like the Romans, with love of their country and of liberty, a zeal for the public good, and a noble emulation of glory, will not be disheartened or dispirited by a succession of unfortunate events. But like them, may we learn by defeat the power of becoming invincible!"[7] An unidentified writer wrote that it was a "day that though so full of sorrow for the Americans, shed so little glory on British arms."[8]

*   *   *

After the major actions, Howe's concern was the state of his army. The victors, to use a term described by Clausewitz in the next century, were at that point in the battle where they were in a state of crisis, a breakdown of order. Howe's army was not the coherent, well-supplied, well-fed and fresh force it had been the night before. His men were disorganized and scattered all over Brooklyn. Grant's troops had been fighting for about ten hours; de Heister's, with the massacre and pursuit to the Old Stone House, were exhausted; and the main column had marched all night and fought a running battle over broken country. Muskets were fouled and ammunition consumed. The troops had not eaten that day and were now burdened by over a thousand prisoners. In the various melees of the morning, even his reserves had been committed.

By contrast, with reinforcements flooding over, Washington had at least 6,000 fresh troops, of various levels of proficiency, behind the lines on Brooklyn Neck. Had these been committed to the battle in a solid mass, supported by heavy cannon from the fortifications in a drive toward the Gowanus, even the superior discipline and firepower of the British units available to meet such an attack might not have been adequate. As noted, during the action at the Old Stone House, Colonel Smallwood had asked Washington for a few regiments to cover the retreat of Stirling's men. Not wishing to gamble with what forces he had left, Washington refused. Had Smallwood made the sortie with the support of the guns of the forts—at the Old Stone House the British had only a few very small cannon—the Battle of Brooklyn might have ended in a draw.

Howe was further beset by a message from the Hessians, who had captured General Sullivan. According to the Germans there might be a large American force, some several thousand strong, somewhere in Brooklyn beyond the main lines. Except for sporadic reports (some

American reinforcements were marching from Hellgate; Miles' regiment had attacked Howe's supply train someplace it should not have been) this intelligence was unconfirmed. But if it were true, it would mean Howe would have to fight a second battle that day, one for which he was not prepared.

Von Heeringen later commented on his high-ranking prisoner: "John Sullivan is a lawyer, and had previously been a servant; but he is a man of genius, whom the rebels will badly miss. He was brought before me. I ordered him to be searched, and found upon his person the original orders of General Washington, from which it was evident that he had the best troops under his command, that everything depended upon maintaining possession of the woods, and that he had 8,000 men."[9]

In any case, Howe saw it as his duty to regroup, feed his troops, attend to prisoners and organize for a siege or perhaps a dawn assault with heavy artillery preparation. Not until all of this had been completed was there any question of exposing the army further. After all, he had Washington bottled up on the edge of Brooklyn, cut off from the mainland, and with siege works growing tighter and more extensive by the hour. And the fleet was ready to beat its way up the East River to isolate the Americans, given the slightest improvement in the weather.

According to his order books, Howe had accomplished all he had planned to do that day. An assault would be too risky. A random advance over ground completely swept by artillery, and subject to accurate fire from American small arms, would have resulted in an unacceptable loss not easily replaced from either England or Germany.

"The [American] lines could not be taken by assault; but by approaches," one British officer wrote. "We had not fascines* to fill ditches, no axes to cut abatis, and no scaling ladders to assault so respectable a work. The lines were a mile and a half in extent, including angles, cannon-proof, with a chain of five redoubts, or rather fortresses with

---

*Before the invention of the sandbag, fascines were the universal military building unit. Consisting of slim tree branches or sapling trunks tied together in bundles about two feet thick, and from 12 to 20 feet long, they were used to protect strong points or for bomb-proof shelters. In a pile they were very effective in stopping small arms fire and absorbing cannon balls.

ditches, as had the lines that formed the intervals; the whole surmount with a most formidable abatis, finished in every part. A corporal and six men [with axes] had a difficulty in getting through the abatis."[10]

According to British military engineers who examined them, the American fortifications were substantial. One Major Holland noted that they were laid out according to the "rules of fortifications," well and solidly built. In his opinion, with a sufficient force and adequate provisions and munitions, they could be held for a long time. A Lieutenant Anbury would later report: ". . . at a small distance from the town are some considerable heights commanding the city of New York. On these is erected a strong and regular fort with four bastions. . . . [The fortifications] are not only on grounds and situations that are extremely advantageous and commanding, but works of great strength, that I am at a loss to account for their so hastily abandoning them, as they were certain by such a step to give up New York."[11]

The American defenses were much more extensive than the hastily erected fieldworks for the Battle of Bunker Hill, June 17, 1775, where Howe suffered 1,054 casualties (226 dead) in his attacking force of 2,250. On the American side, 140 were killed and 271 wounded. Howe, even though he was a major general, commanded the light infantry in person in that battle, and was "for some seconds left along the fiery slope, every officer and man near him having [been] shot down."[12] After the battle he wrote to London: "When I look to the consequences of it, in the loss of so many brave OFFICERS, I do it with horror — THE SUCCESS is too dearly bought."[13] At the time, the British had a force of about 7,000 in Boston.

In their Brooklyn fortifications, the Americans had almost two score cannon — most with greater range and throw weight than the artillery the British had in the field — in five forts connected by entrenchments of a mile-and-a-half front. The afternoon of August 27th, Howe ordered preparations for a formal siege and moved the units in best condition to seal off the American defenses. While half of those troops rested and ate, the other half, 1,300 in all, took up their spades and started digging. Colonel Stephan Kemble wrote: "Wed. Aug 28 & 29. Employed in Erecting Batteries to attack their works on Brookland Heights."[14] Howe also sought to expand his hold on Long Island, sending flying columns of cavalry eastward. It was one of these, a detachment of dragoons*—some say, composed of Loyalists—that captured Brigadier General Nathaniel Woodhull in Jamaica the day after the battle, August 28th.

As individual Americans and fragments of units filtered back across the lines, their forces were regrouped and placed either on the earthworks or in reserve. General Samuel Parsons, who had gone to find Stirling for orders, was cut off and spent the night in a swamp. He found his way back Wednesday via the East River.

That afternoon, emulating the actions of Colonel Hand and his Pennsylvanians a few days earlier against the Hessians, parties of riflemen slipped across the lines of trenches and ranged up to a quarter-mile beyond to fire on any exposed British target. A Lord Harris wrote that his unit was ordered to occupy the edge of a wood opposite the American works: "Exposed to the fire of their riflemen. During the whole evening [of the 27th] they hit but one man, though their balls continually whistled over our heads and lodged in the trees above us."[15]

Those British finished with their duties and not digging trenches sought shelter to rest and recuperate when the baggage train caught up to their positions. They had dinner and cleaned their weapons in readiness for the next engagement, be it in a few minutes or in a few days. Those in the Guards units, when separated from the baggage train, could "pitch their blankets" for shelter. While all British soldiers carried a blanket, the Guards carried ones with a buttonhole and tape in each corner. Like the shelter halves of the 20th-century American Army, these blankets were rigged in pairs, being supported by muskets and ramrods to form a simple "A" tent for four soldiers, the other two blankets being used for bedding.

That same afternoon and evening, as the British dug in and restored themselves, Washington, still convinced his lines could be held, moved in some 4,000 additional troops from Manhattan. This was a gamble since Admiral Howe, had the winds changed, would certainly have moved up the East River and cut off the salient in Brooklyn. No matter how strong the American land fortifications might have been, they never could have sustained concentrated naval bombardment.

---

*Mounted infantry; from the short musket they carried, called in French, *dragon*.

That night and into the next morning, the British kept digging. Wrote Robertson: ". . . this night with a party of 400 men I opened ground opposite their Works and form'd a kind of Paralel (*sic*) or place of Arms* 650 Yards Distant."[16]

While digging, the British also probed the American defenses. "On Wednesday," an American wrote, "in a heavy shower of rain, the enemy attacked our lines between Forts Greene and Putnam. Our men were directed (and readily complied) to lie upon the ground with their bodies over their firelocks [flintlocks, to keep them dry], so that the enemy got repulsed."[17]

As the *New England Chronicle* recorded, some time later: "Wednesday afternoon, a great hail and rain storm came on, attended with thunder and lightening [*sic*]; at which time the ministerial [British] army attacked our lines on L.I., at three different places with the utmost force; but the intrepidity of the soldiers of the United States repulsed them; so that they were obliged immediately to retreat precipitately. The men-of-war at the same time made an attempt to come up to the city, as they did also the day before, but the wind at both times entirely obstructed them."[18]

Private Martin wrote:

The next day [Wednesday] in the afternoon, we had a considerable tight scratch with about an equal number of the British, which began rather unexpectedly, and a little whimsically. A few of our regiment went over the creek, upon business that usually employed us, that is, in search of something to eat. There was [a] field of Indian corn at a short distance from the creek, with several cocks of hay about half way from the creek to the cornfield; the men purposed to get some of the corn, or any thing else that was eatable. When they got up with the haycocks, they were fired upon by an equal number of the British, from the cornfield; our people took to the hay, and the others [the British] to the fence, where they exchanged a number of shots at each other, neither side inclining to give back. A number, say forty or fifty more of our men, went over and drove the British from the fence; they

---

*Place d'Armes, French for a protected assembly place for troops before an assault.

were by this time reinforced in their turn, and drove us back. The two parties kept thus alternately reinforcing, until we had the most of our regiment in the action. After the officers came to command, the English were soon routed from the place, but we dare[d] not follow them for fear of falling into some snare, as the whole British army was in the vicinity of us; I do not recollect that we had any one killed outright, but we had several severely wounded, and some I believe mortally. Our regiment was alone, no other troops being near where we were lying; we were upon a rising ground, covered with a young growth of trees; we felled a fence of trees around us to prevent the approach of the enemies' horse. We lay there a day longer; in the latter part of the afternoon there fell a very heavy shower, which wet us all to the skin, and much damaged our ammunition — about sunset, when the shower had passed over, we were ordered to parade and discharge our pieces. We attempted to fire by platoons for improvement, but we made blundering work of it; it was more like running fire than [volley] firing by divisions; however, we got our muskets as empty as our stomachs, and with half the trouble, nor was it half the trouble to have reloaded them, for we had wherewithal to do that, but not so with our stomachs."[19]

In General Jeremiah Johnson's history of the battle, he wrote: "On the night of the 28th, the British threw up a redoubt on the heights east of Ft. Putnam, from which they opened a fire on the fort; and on the 29th they made a show of attacking the lines. A strong column menaced this on the land of Geo. Powers. The Americans were here prepared to receive them, and orders were issued to reserve their first fire till they could see the whites of their eyes. A few British officers reconnoitered the American lines, when one coming too near was shot by Wm. Van Cott of Bushwick, who then put up his gun and said he had done his part."[20]

The bitterly cold northeast storm that descended on Brooklyn, while pelting the tentless Americans and extinguishing their campfire so they had to eat their ration of biscuits and pickled pork cold, did keep the British fleet from sailing up the channel and eliminating all chance of escape.

As Stephen Olney, of Rhode Island, recalled: "After we got into our fort there came on a dreadful heavy storm with thunder and lightning, and the rain fell in such torrents that the water was soon ankle deep in the fort. With all these inconveniences, and an enemy just without musket-shot, our men could not be kept awake. They would sit down and fall asleep, though Lt. Col. Cornell threatened to make daylight shine through them." Adding to the discouragement was Olney's opinion of the safety of his position: "All that seemed to prevent the enemy taking our main fort was a scarecrow row of palisades from the fort to low water in the cove, which Major [Daniel] Box had set up that morning."[21]

Through Loyalist spies, the British had known that as of the 26th of August this space, between Fort Box and the Gowanus, had not been closed with a fortified line. On the day of the battle one British unit reached the space and seemed surprised to find the new breastwork.

It was still dark and rainy on the morning of Thursday the 29th. The British had finished their siege works and were ready for action. Howe bided his time and did not press on even though the rain stopped and the heavy fog had lifted by noon. During the day there was only desultory firing between the lines.

CHAPTER XII

"This retreat should hold a high place among military transactions"

E VEN THOUGH HIS TROOPS had been demoralized by the loss two
days before and had been exposed to bitter weather for the following
two days and nights, Washington was still of a mind to hold out in
Brooklyn. However, he was finally convinced of the need to save the
army with an evacuation by General Mifflin, Colonel Reed and Colonel
Grayson, who had examined the lines and evaluated what other intelligence they had of the situation. They urged Washington to withdraw
the army before the weather could change and the British sail up the
channel.

The patriots' commander-in-chief held a council of war at his
headquarters in the Cornell house on the afternoon of the 29th with
Generals Putnam, Spencer, Mifflin, McDougal, Parsons, Fellows,
Wadsworth and Scott.* All but revolutionary hard-liner Scott, who had
to be persuaded, favored an immediate withdrawal. The council is
recorded as follows:

---

*John Morin Scott (1730–84), appointed Brigadier General of the New York Militia,
was one of the organizers of the Sons of Liberty, and among the more radical members
of the Provincial Congress. For a short period before the battle he had reverted to civilian
status, becoming a proto-political commissar with the American forces. A ranking
member of the British Secret Service at the time, Paul Wentworth, described Scott as
"an unprincipled, restless, avaricious lawyer, very fit for any intrigue. He will always keep
his own party agitated. . . ."[1]

145

It was submitted to the consideration of the Council, whether, under all circumstances, it would not be eligible to leave Long Island, and its dependencies, and to remove to New York. Unanimously agreed in the affirmative, for the following reasons:

1st. Because our advanced party had met with a defeat, and the wood was lost, where we expected to make a principal stand.

2nd. The great loss sustained in the death or captivity of several valuable officers, and their battalions, or a large portion of them, had occasioned great confusion and discouragement among the troops.

3rd. The heavy rain which fell two days and nights without intermission, had injured the arms, and spoiled a great part of the ammunition; and the soldiery, being without cover, and obliged to lay in the lines, were worn out, and it was to be feared would not be retained in them by any order.

4th. From the time the army moved from Flatbush, several large ships had endeavored to get up, as supposed into the East River, to cut off our communications (by which the whole army would have been destroyed), but, the wind being N.E., could not effect it.

5th. Upon consulting with persons of knowledge of the harbor, they were of opinion that small ships might come between Long Island and Governor's Island, where there are no obstructions, and which would cut off the communication effectually; and who were also of opinion that hulks sunk between Governor's Island and the city of New York were no sufficient security for obstructing the passage.

6th. Though our lines were fortified by some strong redoubts, yet a great part of them were weak, being abattied with brush, and affording no strong cover—so that there was reason to apprehend they might be forced, which would put our troops in confusion, and, having no retreat, they must have been cut to pieces or made prisoners.

7th. The divided state of the troops renders our defence very precarious, and the duty of defending long and extensive lines in so many different places, without proper conveniences and cover, so very fatiguing, that the troops had become dispirited by their incessant duty and watching.

8th. Because the enemy had sent several ships of war into the Sound, to a place called Flushing Bay; and, from the information received that a part of their troops was moving across Long Island, that way, there was reason to apprehend they meant to pass over land, and form an encampment above Kingsbridge [on Harlem Creek] in order to cut off and prevent all communication between our army and the country beyond them, or get in our rear.[2]

Orders were issued to collect everything that could float to transport the army. As luck would have it, part of the American forces just arrived in Brooklyn were composed of fishermen from Massachusetts: Colonel John Glover's Marblehead Regiment and the 27th Massachusetts, of soldiers from Lynn, Salem and Danvers, led by Israel Hutchinson. These men had spent their lives, from the time they were big enough to handle an oar, rowing the dories of the Massachusetts Bay fisheries. The uniforms of the Marblehead men, in fact, consisted of short blue coats and white duck trousers — not unlike the uniform of the British Navy.

Giving the impression that he proposed to ferry part of the army to land at Hallet's Point to the north on the East River and outflank the British, Washington began the evacuation. General Mifflin was given command of the covering forces — the best units Washington had — to hold the fortified lines, while the rest of the army, its supplies and guns escaped. The rearguard included Shee's and Magaw's Pennsylvanians, Chester's Connecticut Continentals, Haslet's Delaware Regiment, the remnants of Smallwood's Marylanders and Colonel Lasher's 1st New York. The New York unit's 120 grenadiers were each issued six hand grenades in addition to their other arms and were to act as a rapid-response force to repulse any breach in the lines.

In the ranks of any army, rumor and speculation fly faster than fact. Private Martin's narrative continued, for the 29th:

Just at dusk, I, with one or two others of our company, went off to a barn, about half a mile distant, with intent to get some straw to lodge upon, the ground and leaves being drenched with water, and we as wet as they; it was quite dark, in the barn, and while I was fumbling about the floor, someone called to me from the top of the mow, inquiring where I was from; I told him. He asked me if we had not had an engagement there (having heard us discharge our guns); I told him we had, and a severe one too; he asked if many were killed; I told him that I saw none killed, nor any very badly wounded. I then hear several others, as it appeared, speaking on the mow. Poor fellows, they had better have been at their posts, than skulking in a barn on account of a little wet, for I have not the least doubt but that the British had possession of their mortal parts before the noon of next day. I could not find any straw, but found some wheat in the sheaf, standing by the side of the floor; I took a sheaf or two and returned as fast as I could to the regiment.

When I arrived the men were all paraded to march off the ground; I left my wheat, seized my musket, and fell into the ranks. We were strictly enjoined not to speak, or even cough, while on the march. All orders were given from officer to officer, and communicated to the men in whispers. What such secrecy could mean we could not divine. We marched off in the same way we had come on the Island, forming various conjectures among ourselves as to our destination. Some were of the opinion that we were to endeavor to get on the flank or the rear of the enemy. Others, that we were going up the East River, to attack them in that quarter; but none, it seems, knew the right of the matter. We marched on, however, until we arrived at the ferry, where we immediately embarked on board the batteaux (*sic*) [rowboats] and were conveyed safely to New-York, where we were landed about three o'clock in the morning, nothing against our inclinations.[3]

The evacuation, begun after dark, at about 8:00 P.M., was managed by Brigadier General McDougal. It began slowly with the Massachusetts soldiers manning the oars. Later, a wind blew away the fog and, as sails were hoisted, the transfer of troops and equipment speeded up. At first, ammunition, cannon, horses and baggage were transferred. The larger guns, which were mounted on naval carriages, were too cumbersome to be easily moved through the deep mud and were spiked — split nails or files were driven into their touch holes to disable them — and left behind. Next, the reserves and, finally, at about 10:00 P.M., the troops from the forward positions began withdrawing. Stephen Olney reported: "On our retreat to N.Y., we had to take our baggage, camp-equipage, &c. on our shoulders to the boats, and tedious was the operation through mud and mire."[4]

Throughout the evening, into the night and until dawn, line after line of cold, wet, defeated American soldiers filed down to the shore to be ferried to Manhattan. In many cases, they went quietly and in some in a state of near panic to escape. The value of eyewitness reports can vary greatly, especially in the confusion of battle or its immediate aftermath, and depend on one's viewpoint and point of view. One Tory saw groups that panicked: "Matters were in such confusion at the ferry . . . [to] get within a quarter of a mile of the ferry, the rebel crowd was so great, and they were in such trepidation that those in the rear were mounting on the shoulders and clambering over the heads of those before them."[5]

According to Colonel Fish, one of Washington's aides, there was disorder bordering on panic early in the evacuation. Washington, Fish related, was infuriated by some men who were fighting their way onto the boats. He picked up a large stone, and holding it above his head, ordered the men to leave the boat or he "would sink it to hell."[6] Word of Washington's action spread, Fish said, and order prevailed in most cases during the evacuation.

Colonel Smallwood noted that panic occurred among some New England units, reporting that the evacuation "was happily completed under cover of a thick fog and a southwest wind, both which favored our retreat, otherwise the fear, disorder, and confusion of some of the eastern troops must have retarded and discovered our retreat and subjected numbers to be cut off."[7]

Order generally prevailed, however, and the Massachusetts fishermen rowed with muffled, cloth-covered oars through the night in their endless two-mile circuit from shore to shore. One Marblehead man recalled making eleven round trips.

Major Benjamin Tallmadge, adjutant with Colonel John Chester's Connecticut regiment, wrote of the withdrawal: "To move so large a body of troops with all their necessary appendages across a river full a mile wide, with a rapid current, in face of a victorious, well-disciplined army nearly three times as numerous as his own and a fleet capable of stopping the navigation so that not one boat could have passed over, seemed to present most formidable obstacles. But in the face of these difficulties, the Commander-in-Chief so arranged his business that on the evening of the twenty-ninth by ten o'clock, the troops began to retire from the lines, but as one regiment left their station or guard, the remaining troops moved to the right and left and filled up the vacancies, while General Washington took his station at the ferry and super-intended the embarkation of the troops."[8]

To cover the evacuated lines, Washington gave General Mifflin two Pennsylvania battalions, one of which was commanded by Colonel Hand. All went well until two in the morning, when, as Hand commented:

> Alexander Scammell, acting aide to Washington, told General Mifflin "that the boats were waiting, and the Commander-in-Chief anxious for the arrival of the troops at the ferry." General Mifflin said he thought he must be mistaken, that he could not imagine the General could mean the troops he immediately commanded. Scammell replied that he was not mistaken, adding that he came from the extreme left, had ordered all the troops he had met to march; that in consequence they were then in motion and that he would go on and give the same orders. General Mifflin then ordered me to call my advance pickets and sentinels, to collect and form my regiment, and to march as soon as possible, and quitted me.
>
> I obeyed, but had not gone far before I perceived the front had halted, and, hastening to inquire the cause, I met the Com-mander-in-Chief, who . . . said "Is not that Colonel Hand . . . ?"
>
> His Excellency said he was surprised at me in particular, that he did not expect I would have abandoned my post. I answered that I had not abandoned it, and I had marched by order of my immediate commanding officer. He said it was impossible. I told him I hoped, if I could satisfy him I had the orders of General Mifflin, he would not think me particularly to blame . . .
>
> General Mifflin just then coming up, and asking what the matter was, His Excellency said: "Good God! General Mifflin, I am afraid you have ruined us by so unseasonably withdrawing the troops from the lines."

General Mifflin replied with some warmth: "I did it by your order."

His Excellency declared it could not be.

General Mifflin swore: "By God, I did," and asked: "Did Scammell act as an aide-de-camp for the day, or did he not?"

His Excellency acknowledged that he did.

"Then!" said Mifflin, "I had orders through him."

The General replied it was a dreadful mistake, and informed him that matters were in such confusion at the ferry, and unless we could resume our posts before the enemy discovered we had left them, in all probability the most disagreeable consequences would follow. We immediately returned, and had the good fortune to recover our former stations, and keep them for some hours longer, without the enemy perceiving what was going forward."9

That evening, a Tory, Mrs. John Rapalie, sent her black slave through the lines to alert the British of the evacuation. He was intercepted by Hessians who spoke no English and could not understand the slave's Dutch. It was not until late in the morning that he delivered the message to an English officer.

The evacuation continued through the night. One American soldier recorded: "The brigades were ordered to be in readiness with bag and baggage to march, but knew not where or for what; the 2d did not know where the 1st had gone; nor the 3d, the 2d. The last marched off at the firing of the 3 o'clock gun on Friday morning. The night was remarkably still, the water smooth as glass, so that all our boats went over safe, though many were but about 3 inches out of the water. At sunrise a great fog came up. We left half a dozen large guns. 3 or 4 men were missing who came off in a batteau."10

Tallmadge wrote: "As the dawn approached, those of us who remained in the trenches became very anxious for our safety, at which time there were several regiments still on duty, and a dense fog began to rise, and seemed to settle over both encampments; so dense was the atmosphere, that a man could not be discerned six yards off. [At first light] we had orders to leave the lines, but before we reached the ferry the regiment was ordered back again. Col. Chester faced about and

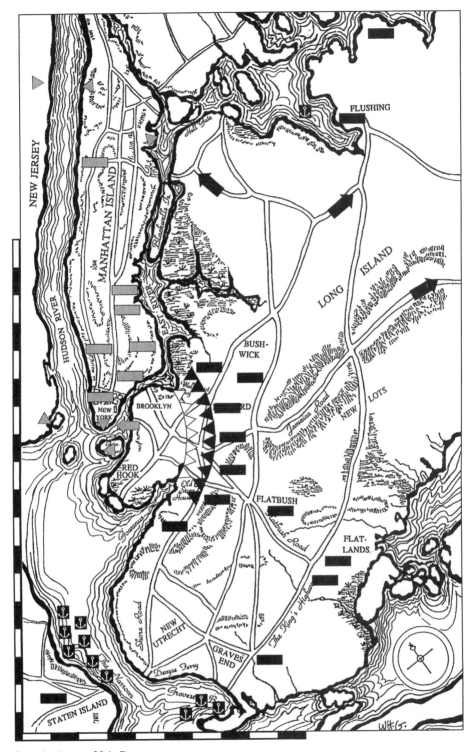

Saturday August 30th, Dawn

returned to the lines, where the regiment tarried till the sun had risen, but the fog remained as dense as ever. Finally a second order came, and we joyfully bid those trenches a long adieu. When we reached Brooklyn ferry the boats had not yet returned from their last trip, but they soon appeared . . ."[11]

The crossing made, Tallmadge noted: "I had left my horse at the ferry, tied to a post. The troops having all safely reached N.Y., and the fog continuing thick as ever, I got leave to return with a crew of volunteers for my favorite horse. I had got off with him some distance into the river before the enemy appeared in Brooklyn [at the landing]. As soon as they reached the ferry we were saluted merrily from their musketry, and finally by their field-pieces."[12]

The fog that had covered the troops' movement lifted as the sun rose on Friday, August 30th, and the British did not suspect anything unusual happening until seven o'clock that morning. Nonetheless, the suspicion was not confirmed until General Robertson led a party into the deserted camp at 8:30, just as the boats were taking the last of the Americans to Manhattan.

Colonel Kemble wrote: "In A.M. to our great astonishment found they had evacuated all their works on Brookland & Red Hook without a shot being fired at them & to the best of our observation found a body of 300 or 400 remaining on Governor's Island who might have been taken by flat Boat, but for what reason was not attempted. Neither could our shipping get up for want of wind, and the whole escaped the following Night to New York."[13]

When the British occupied Fort Stirling, they immediately unspiked the guns there and turned them on the boats of the last fleeing Americans. Though no hits were scored with the cannon, the British did capture three Americans who had apparently stayed behind to loot. "It was one of the most anxious, busy nights I ever recollect," Tallmadge wrote, "and in being the third in which hardly any of us had closed our eyes in sleep, we were all greatly fatigued."[14]

As noted by one British military critic: "Those who are best acquainted with the difficulty, embarrassment, noise and tumult which attended even by day, and with no enemy at hand, a movement of this nature . . . will be the first to acknowledge that this retreat should hold a high place among military transactions."[15]

As a result of this retreat, Washington was able to extricate about 9,500 men, his entire force, with their equipment and supplies, and all but five cannon from under the noses of the British. Major Tallmadge, in one of the final boats, wrote of his seeing a very tall man, in a cloak and boots, coming down the steps to be helped board a skiff by one of the men from Marblehead. It was Washington, who left with the last of his troops.

CHAPTER XIII

After "The Fox"

H OWE'S REPORT ON THE BATTLE reached England on October 10th and was received with "an extravagance of joy"[1] in the Royal Court. He was awarded the Order of the Bath, at the time one of Britain's most exclusive military orders, limited to 36 living members.

Closer to the scene, however, feelings were different. Many on the British side condemned Howe's lack of aggressive pursuit of the rebels, on the day of the battle, as well as later, delaying the follow-up in taking Manhattan Island. Sir George Collier, captain of the *Rainbow,* sarcastically summed up the feelings of the bitterest:

The having to deal with a generous, merciful, *forbearing* enemy, who would take no unfair *advantages,* must surely have been highly satisfactory to General Washington, and he was certainly very deficient in not expressing his gratitude to General Howe for his *kind* behavior towards him. Far from taking the rash resolution of *hasty passing* over the East River...and *crushing at once* a frightened, trembling enemy, [Howe] generously gave them time to recover from their panic—to throw up *fresh works*—to make new arrangements—and to recover from the torpid state the rebellion appeared in from its late shock.

For *many succeeding* days did our brave veterans, consisting of twenty-two thousand men, stand on the banks of the East River, like Moses on Mount Pisgah, looking at their promised land, little more than a half a mile distant. The rebels' standards waved insolently in the air from many different quarters of New York. The British troops could scarcely contain their indignation at the sight and at their own *inactivity*; the officers were *displeased and amazed,* not being able to account for the strange delay.[2]

Even General Clinton noted that if pursuit had been allowed, "Not a man would have escaped."[3]

Captain Frederick Mackenzie, of the 23rd Regiment, was more moderate: "Many are of opinion that [Howe] should have followed up the advantage he gained on the 27th of August and either on that day or the following attacked the Rebels in their lines at Brooklyn, yet it must be allowed that it was extremely proper in him to consider what fatal consequences might have attended a check which the Army might have received in the first action of the campaign."[4]

For his part, Howe believed it would have been "Inconsiderate and even criminal"[5] to have made a frontal assault with the Americans surrounded on land and, he hoped, cut off by British ships on the river. Now, of course, the Americans had escaped from the edge of one island to the tip of another. But the British still had superior forces in the area.

Washington's reaction to the battle was shared by many others on his side: "Till of late, I had no doubt in my own mind of defending this place."[6] With the army having gotten across from Brooklyn, however, it seems that he was reevaluating his original strategic decision to defend New York. The British Navy had already mounted one amphibious operation that nearly resulted in the destruction of the American army — and only unfavorable weather had kept warships from blocking the American retreat. In the future, the best hopes for the Revolutionary forces would be found farther inland, or at least away from a city surrounded by navigable waterways.

*   *   *

In New York, on September 5th, a British party under flag of truce delivered a list of 148 American officers taken prisoner who asked for the baggage and cash they had left with friends to be sent them.

Despite his opinion in July that "peace will not be restored in

America until the Rebel Army is defeated,"[7] Howe delayed his pursuit of the retreating Continental Army for about two weeks in the hopes that an informal peace conference could be called to discuss a reconciliation. Generals Sullivan and Stirling, who had been taken prisoner, were chosen to act as intermediaries and set up the meeting. In captivity they had been treated civilly by Howe, who dined with them regularly, and they had given their parole as officers and gentlemen to act honorably in this mission of peace. They went to the Continental Congress in Philadelphia to request the conference.

The meeting was arranged and held on September 11th in Tottenville on Staten Island in the Billopp Manor, now the Conference House (a restored monument to the Revolution). In attendance were the Howes, Benjamin Franklin, John Adams and Edmund Rutledge. The American delegates, however, would not accept a demand that the Declaration of Independence be revoked, and so the meeting broke up. The British resumed their advance, crossing the East River on September 15th.

During the delay, the British had consolidated their hold, establishing garrison posts the length of Long Island, with a fort at Willett's Point (the site today of Fort Totten) to control the entrance to the East River from Long Island Sound. They set up cannon in today's Astoria and on Blackwell's (now Roosevelt) Island in preparation for their anticipated crossing to Manhattan.

On September 6th, a new weapon of war had meanwhile made its debut, however inauspicious. That night, a whaleboat towed a hand-powered submarine, *The American Turtle*, invented by David Bushnell of Connecticut, across New York Bay toward the British fleet. Piloted by Sergeant Ezra Lee, it submerged and approached Admiral Howe's flagship, the *Eagle*. Lee found, however, that he could not drill into the ship's copper-clad hull to attach a gunpowder bomb, and had to return to New York at dawn. Despite the lack of success, this was the first recorded use of an operational submarine, one that could submerge, navigate under water and then resurface (earlier designs had been deficient in the last quality).

In the days following the battle, as British cavalry swept the length of Long Island, the residents were torn in their feelings. The concerns of those who supported the American cause were perhaps best summed up by Reverend Woodhull, writing to his wife: "Poor Long Island: I know what will become of my relations there. May God help them. They were left to the mercy of the cruel enemy."[8]

Loyalist sentiments were shown, however, by many in the heretofore rebel bastion of Suffolk County. When Howe suggested to the people of Suffolk that, should they wish to demonstrate their loyalty, they send 200 wagons to help in moving the British Army's baggage from New Utrecht to Hellgate, they responded by sending 300.

In the middle of September, Howe conducted another successful landing operation, this time on Manhattan Island. Once again, Washington had misdeployed his army: he had placed his best troops at the southern tip of the island and on the heights to the northwest in the great citadel of Fort Washington. He left the approaches from the East River defended by his weakest units, composed mostly of militiamen.

In the weeks since the evacuation, Washington's command had hemorrhaged as many of his summer soldiers chose to return home. One instance was the Connecticut militia, which went from 8,000 after the Battle of Brooklyn to about 2,000 in the first week of September. Nonetheless, he reorganized, creating three "Grand Divisions." Putnam's, with 5,000, was stationed in a New York City turned in the past few months into an armed camp. Its streets were closed with barricades and its strategic points—elevations, crossroads—all had their artillery redoubts. Additionally, as of the time of the Battle of Brooklyn, Manhattan had become Washington's chief depot for military stores.

Contrary to the dispositions in Brooklyn, where he kept his most indifferent units behind the strong fortified lines, Washington placed his strongest, Heath's division of 9,000 men, in the fortified complex on the heights between Harlem and King's Bridge. This force, with Haslet's Delawares and what was left of Smallwood's Marylanders, worked constantly to strengthen the works, a two-mile-long complex of strong points centered around Fort Washington.

In the center of this dispersement, which ran from the Battery to the heights of what is Riverdale in today's Bronx—some 16 miles—Washington placed his least trained and organized, and most poorly equipped, division. While this force of 6,000 (five brigades) was comprised primarily of militia units, it did have the advantage of being commanded by one of the best American generals, Nathanael Greene, recently recovered from camp fever. However, it was spread more or less evenly along the length of the East River to prevent a British landing. This deployment was an effort to have troops on hand wherever Howe might descend along the eight- to ten-mile stretch of shoreline. Howe had the choice of assembling his landing craft out of sight in the Newtown Creek on the border of Queens and Brooklyn, or behind the two-mile stretch of Blackwell's Island, which extends between 49th and 85th Streets, its West Channel between it and Manhattan only about 300 yards wide.

On September 10th, Howe made his first advance, taking Montresor's — now Randall's — Island, at the juncture of Harlem Creek and the East River. It had been set up as a camp for American soldiers suffering from yellow fever. Howe learned through his intelligence that it was lightly guarded. From this spot he could threaten the Morrisiana Estate (today's South Bronx) across the north fork of the Harlem — a walk when the tide was low (even today), that might not wet the soldiers'shoes. Or he could, using 100 men, in ten minutes, bridge the main channel of the Harlem with fascines and march on King's Bridge, only six miles away, to cut off Manhattan.

A few days after the taking of this strategic point, the Americans had made an ineffectual (read "disastrous") attempt to retake Montresor. The landing party was small, fitting into only three boats. The lead boat, with the commander, landed first, came under heavy fire and was abandoned by the others, which immediately withdrew, leaving the leading party to be killed or captured.

At a council of war on September 12th, Greene had raised objections to Washington's positioning of the three "Grand Divisions." It was decided to concentrate the army around Fort Washington as soon as the large quantity of military stores could be withdrawn to the north from the city. The motion was carried by a vote of ten to three, the dissenters labeled in Alexander McDougall's diary as "a fool, a knave, and an honest, obstinate man" — respectively, Generals Joseph Spencer, George Clinton and William Heath.[9]

On September 15th, Howe sent three frigates and an armed

schooner to run the gauntlet of the Hudson batteries to a station north of Fort Washington. This diversion presented the threat of a landing and also cut American communications across the river from New Jersey.

On the other side of Manhattan, at Kip's Bay (where today's 34th Street meets the East River), the frigates *Phoenix, Roebuck* and *Rose,* with two smaller warships, anchored 200 yards off the shore and opened a one-hour barrage on the American positions at 11 A.M. The short-range bombardment by the 70-gun broadside was initially answered by desultory fire, which trailed off as the American batteries were taken out of action, either by hostile fire or withdrawal. These American defenses were, according to Private Martin: "Nothing more than a ditch along the bank of the river with the dirt thrown out towards the water."[10]

At 1:00 P.M., 84 flatboats, which had assembled in Newton Creek out of sight of American observers, landed 4,000 British and Hessian troops under Clinton, who set up his headquarters in a farmhouse on Murray Hill. An advance force was sent to where the New York Public Library now stands on 42nd Street, and von Donop took his three Hessian Grenadier battalions south to about 14th Street to be in a position to attack Putnam in lower Manhattan. All of Howe's first division waited in place until the second wave, some 9,000 men, could be landed and brought into action.

The American militia units facing the landing bolted and Greene was unable to control them. Washington, who had ridden from his headquarters in Harlem Heights on hearing the naval bombardment, found the line disintegrating, with men ". . . retreating with the utmost *precipitation* . . . flying in every direction and in the utmost confusion notwithstanding the efforts of their generals to form them. I used every means in my power to rally and get them in order, but my attempts were fruitless and ineffectual and on the appearance of a small party of the enemy, not more than sixty or seventy in number, their disorder increased and they ran away without firing a shot."[11]

According to witnesses, Washington hurled his hat on the ground and said either: "Good God, have I got such troops as these?" or, "Are these the men with which I am to defend America?"[12] In any case, the commander-in-chief soon found himself and his aides practically alone, surrounded only by a jumble of litter and equipment, abandoned by troops who did not want their flight encumbered.

This was the moment when Washington showed his greatest despair in public. In his passion he was reckless and rode near the British lines, tempting capture or a marksman's bullet. Greene rode next to him, pleading for the general to turn back. Finally, an aide grabbed the bridle of Washington's horse and pointed him in the direction of safety.

Israel Putnam, at the tip of Manhattan, knew the British had landed and ordered an immediate retreat to Harlem Heights along the shortest way, called the Post Road—the path that today follows Lexington Avenue. His knowledge of the geography of Manhattan Island was better than it had been of Brooklyn, but his intelligence was as bad as during the earlier battle. Howe, with 13,000 troops, sat astride Putnam's proposed route in Murray Hill.

Aaron Burr, Putnam's aide, intervened, convincing the general to move up Broadway and its extension, the Bloomingdale Road, which ran diagonally north toward the Hudson. The withdrawal was hasty, however, and included only supplies that could be moved easily; the heavier cannon plus cumbersome camp implements, including large cooking kettles, were abandoned. In this movement the Americans passed only a few hundred yards from the British, the heavy forest concealing each body of troops from the other.

Thanks mainly to Howe's slow and deliberate movements—his order books note that occupying Murray Hill and regrouping was all he had planned for that part of the day—the Americans had time to make their retreat.

Howe's tarrying, on the other hand, gave rise to one of the more charming myths of the American Revolution, that of Mrs. Murray's Madeira. Mary Lindley Murray, whose husband, Robert, was away (either as a colonel with the American Army on Long Island or not, the family being Quaker), was alone in her farmhouse with her twelve children. It has been reported that she invited Howe and his staff in for re-freshments—cakes and wine—and delayed the British advance for two hours, guaranteeing the American escape. Nevertheless, even after a two-hour delay, the bulk of Putnam's command was still trying to escape from New York.

In a few days Howe secured the city, only to contend with a fire on September 20th and 21st, which destroyed some 560 houses, or one-eighth of those he had counted on for winter quarters. The cause of the fire was never determined, but Washington wrote: "Providence, or some good honest fellow, has done more for us than we were disposed to do for ourselves."[13] Earlier, the Continental Congress had forbidden the burning of New York in the event of an American retreat.

It was following the fire, on the night of September 21st, that Captain Nathan Hale was captured. He had infiltrated New York via Long Island and Brooklyn. Found in civilian clothes and with papers containing information on the British dispositions, he was hanged, without a trial, on the 22nd. Before execution, he wrote to his brother a letter that contained the famous words: "I only regret I have but one life to lose for my country" — not knowing his brother had been killed in action the week before.

*   *   *

After the landing in and occupation of New York, Howe pressed up the island, meeting the Americans again — and being stopped for the first time by them — at the battle of Harlem Heights on September 16th. This was a heavy skirmish that began in a buckwheat field at about where 120th Street is today, between Broadway and Riverside Drive. A party of about 150 Americans under Lieutenant Colonel Thomas Knowlton had crossed the Hollow Way, a gully to the south of what is now West 125th Street, and climbed Vanderwater's Heights (later the site of Columbia University). They came across two light infantry battalions and a detachment from the Black Watch. Faced with this large force, the patriots pulled back in good order. According to Washington's aide, Colonel Joseph Reed, just then the British sounded a bugle call meant for the entire force of Americans to hear: "In the most insulting manner. . . as is usual after a fox chase. . . . I never felt such a sensation before, it seemed to crown our disgrace." Reed believed the withdrawal that had just occurred was yet another American retreat.[14]

The British had a different version of the story. Over the previous few weeks, they had consistently won the engagements, but never decisively, and always with Washington escaping at the last moment.

Washington's elusiveness had earned him the nickname "The Fox." At Harlem Heights, Washington was only a short distance behind Reed, but out of the latter's sight. When the commander was spotted by the British, instead of sounding the regulation "Charge!" on the hunting horn then commonly used for signaling, one British bugler sounded "Tally-ho!" — traditionally a signal that a fox had been sighted.

The Americans under Knowlton had actually withdrawn only a short distance and were joined by another 150 men, from General John Nixon's brigade. They counterattacked, driving the British back a few hundred yards. One British prisoner was reported saying: ". . . they were never more surprised than to see [the Americans] advancing to attack them"; he had expected the Americans "would have run away as they did the day before."[15] The British lost 100 killed, but the Americans could not hold the position and had to make a strategic retreat back up Harlem Heights. Nonetheless, Washington's confidence was restored: "This little advantage has inspired our troops *prodigiously*. . . . They find that it only requires resolution and good officers to make an enemy (that they stood in too much dread of) give way."[16]

It took Howe a month to consolidate his position in New York. On the 12th of October a force led by Clinton landed at Throg's Neck (the site of today's Fort Schuyler Park in the Bronx) and was bottled up until another landing was made at Pell's Point, three miles north, on the 18th. The two landings were planned as drives north toward New Rochelle and eventually White Plains, and west to cut off the garrison at the Fort Washington complex. The British occupied the crossing of Harlem Creek at King's Bridge on October 22nd. But the drive to the north was slowed by Colonel John Glover and 750 Massachusetts men with three cannon. This action is commemorated on a plaque on a large rock in Pelham Bay Park.

The British fought and won the Battle of White Plains on October 28. Washington withdrew five miles farther north and Howe, instead of following up his success, once more turned his attention to Fort Washington.

Located at about where 184th Street is in Washington Heights, the citadel was perched on a 230-foot-high hill. Its approaches were protected by rocky slopes and the western one secured by almost vertical cliffs rising above the Hudson River. Having isolated the position, Howe landed 3,000 Germans under General von Knyphausen at Spuyten Duyvil Creek to the north. From the east, the attack was carried out by Lord Percy, and Cornwallis pressed from the south, all being preceded by artillery bombardment. (Just as there were a number of Generals Clinton in the theater, there was more than one Stirling. A Colonel Stirling of the Black Watch distinguished himself in this action.)

After the assaults on the 15th and 16th of November, Fort Washington fell, with 53 Americans dead and 2,818 captured, as well as the loss of 146 cannon, 12,000 cannon rounds, 2,800 muskets and 400,000 cartridges.

*   *   *

As the fighting moved farther away from Long Island, a sense of guarded relief grew among the Dutch in Brooklyn. Many, who had been indifferent to politics, suddenly became ardent Royalists: women wore red ribbons; men, red patches on their hats; and even slaves managed to display patches of scarlet rags. For the men, however, wearing a red patch had a double significance. It was in part support of the British and in part a sign of distinction from the many rebel prisoners who were on parole and billeted in farmhouses all over Brooklyn. This visible display of affection for the Crown, it is said, caused red flannel petticoats to be in short supply, so many having been used to make Royalist badges.

After the battle, the family brewery of the Livingstons was named the King's Brewery, the Ferry House Tavern became the King's Head, and the Flatlands racetrack was renamed Ascot Heath.

Manhattan had been depleted to about 5,000 souls because of its inhabitants' fleeing first the Americans, then the British, or simply the fighting. A surge in its population began again, however, as Tories fled American-controlled areas, until by war's end the population totaled over 30,000. James Rivington, publisher of the *New York Gazette*, a longtime Loyalist newspaper, sent one of his two presses across the Hudson to American-held Newark, which allowed him to publish simultaneously Tory and Whig editions.

On Long Island some militia units raised to fight for the American cause were persuaded to take an oath of loyalty to the Crown, and hundreds of Long Islanders joined newly formed Loyalist units. Like their fellows on Staten Island, who changed sides the day after Howe stepped ashore, these formations were promised they would only be needed to serve on Long Island.

CHAPTER XIV

"The next Augustan Age will dawn on the other side of the Atlantic"

I N THE BATTLE OF BROOKLYN, the American Army performed remarkably well considering all its problems. Despite overwhelming British superiority in troops, organization, discipline and weaponry, the enemy was unable to force the choke points at Battle Pass and on the Shore Road until the Americans were surrounded and vastly outnumbered.

The armies of both sides each showed a considerable unity of purpose. Aside from frustration among British officers over what they perceived as Howe's inaction, there is no record of disaffection in either camp. None of the contemporary writers cast blame. There were no stories of jealousy or hatred among officers on either side. Possibly because they were too busy fighting the British, the Americans rallied behind Washington; the British, professionals to the core, got on with the job.

Militarily, to some who are acquainted with modern armies, one fact stands out: the ability to move quickly and supply large masses of troops at that time seems almost miraculous. In four hours Howe moved 14,000 troops and over 40 cannon, weighing an average of 1,200 pounds apiece, across the New York Narrows by rowboat and without losing a man. Within ten minutes of the landing, as many as 4,000 men were in formation and beginning to move inland. On the day of the battle de Heister sent about 2,000 Highlanders from Flatbush Road to reinforce Grant near the foot of Green-Wood Cemetery. This movement took about the same amount of time as it does today for a family to travel the route by bus. Howe marched 14,000 men and 28 cannon nine miles in the dark during his flanking movement, along a rutted and muddy path seldom more than 12 feet wide. Later that year, Cornwallis crossed the Hudson River with 4,000 to 6,000 men, marched six miles and captured (newly renamed) Fort Lee; the next day he did 25 more miles. In April 1777, William Tryon, now with the military command he always preferred, crossed Long Island Sound with 2,000 infantry, supported by cavalry, and marched 23 miles in one day from Fairfield to Danbury, Connecticut. After burning the city and the miltary stores it contained, he fought his way back to the Sound, 27 miles this time, in one day, inflicting more casualties on the Americans who tried to stop him than he himself suffered.

Washington's evacuation from Brooklyn was a military phenom- enon unequaled even in most peacetime practice maneuvers. Including the three looters the British captured, casualties and damages among his 9,000-plus men amounted to a trifle of the percentage of losses acceptable for even a training exercise.

The story of the Battle of Brooklyn is simple. In the first major trial of the American Army with the forces of the British Empire, the rebels, with no thought-out concept of battle, were outmaneuvered and lost. The heroism of Stirling and the Marylanders, however, showed that the Americans were a force to be reckoned with in this, the first major encounter in what would be an endless succession of bloodshed in democratic wars to come. The practical, sensible professional soldier of the 18th century was passing into history. It would be an age of the "patriot" fighting for the "patriotic cause" from now on. American citizen soldiers stood up to the professionals of the British Army and professionals from the German states who were there to fill the coffers of their princelings. Many patriots served in Brooklyn behind the lines, but not too far behind, cut off by a river the British fleet could control once the winds shifted and the tides changed. They were prepared, or resigned, to do as much as those under direct fire. John Glover and

Israel Hutchinson, with their amphibious troops, volunteered for a fight that few could relish, and showed their own brand of heroism in the evacuation.

The loss of Long Island had immediate repercussions on the larger stage of world events. Under the urging of his Secretary of Foreign Affairs, King Louis XVI of France had been on the verge of recognizing the young nation — until news of the defeat reached him. Even though military supplies had started trickling into American ports from France, it was not until the American victory at Saratoga, in October 1777, that the climate in the court at Versailles changed. On February 6, 1778, the French signed a treaty formally recognizing the United Colonies. In July of that year a French fleet, under Vice Admiral Charles Hector, Comte d'Estaing, with four thousand French regulars aboard, arrived off Sandy Hook to actively support the American cause.

The imbalance of forces on the day of the battle, compounded by the continued aggravation of the colonies' insistence on short-term service, helped convince the Continental Congress to answer Washington's pleas for a standing army, at least for the duration of the war. Well before the Battle of Brooklyn, in January 1776, the Congress had authorized 26 infantry regiments and one regiment each of artillery and riflemen for the Continental Army. These units were similar in strength to their corresponding British regiments (a total of 20,373, according to organizational charts). Shortly after the battle, the Congress voted the recruiting of an additional 88 battalions, the soldiers to serve for the length of the war. Organized on the new, heavy American Continental plan, these battalions, although nominally units smaller than regiments, were equal in manpower to the British regiments they would face.

For Washington, the Battle of Brooklyn began a series of retreats and holding actions in Manhattan, Westchester and New Jersey — a sort of latter-day anabasis, or "journey upward," starting with an ill-formed army and learning from his defeats. The tide would turn for the young republic on a December night in Trenton, when Washington crossed the Delaware River and regained the offensive — decisively defeating the same Hessians who had triumphed over him in Brooklyn and Manhattan.

Indeed, the birth of the United Colonies would be viewed by many at the time as one of classic dimension; writers comparing it — this first republic in two thousand years — with the struggles of the Greek city states and the Roman republic, adding, for good measure, the glory of the Roman Empire under Augustus Caesar, whose rule provided peace, stability and wealth to countries ranging from Egypt to England. In 1775, Hugh Walpole already had offered a glimpse of America's future when, in a letter to Sir Horace Mann, he wrote, "The next Augustan Age will dawn on the other side of the Atlantic."[1]

* * *

The war continued for five more years and peace came two years thereafter, with no more bloody engagement than that which was fought beside the Gowanus and in the pass farther up the hill that August day in 1776. The seeds of the new "democratic warfare" were sown; they burst open with the massive armies and devastating battles of the French Revolution not long after.

The French officers who had served during the war in America — men like the young Marquis de Lafayette — took home with them tactics that would be applied by the French Revolutionary Army. With the return to Europe, too, of British and Hessian officers, the ideas of skirmishing, a looser line of battle with only two ranks, and faster movements on the battlefield began to take hold in the armies of Europe. Cornwallis, seeing in 1785 the maneuvers of the Prussian Army under Frederick the Great — once the exemplar of military practice — considered them "Such as the worst General in England (after their American experience) would be hooted at for practising."[2]

With the absence of conscription, today the United States has gone back to an 18th-century idea of the "professional army," at least in theory if not in scope. *Then,* the artisans and members of the middle class, who were producing, tax-paying members of society, were generally exempt from military service; *today,* instead of excess nobility as officers (and, as rank and file, the lower orders), the excess of the nation's managerial classes become officers, and the enlisted personnel are, in great percentage, recruited as volunteers from the poor and working classes. Many of these new recruits are attracted by the opportunities they find in the military, which can be far better than what are available in civilian life.

The advent of democracy brought the military more prominently into the political process. In past centuries, it had been maintained as a neutral instrument of the state. Its rank and file were politically disenfranchised and were generally isolated from the population at large. In the higher echelons, the military could only advise the government and carry out, as best it could, the objectives set down for it by the state. Although it may be viewed on the surface as feudal elitism, the disdain shown by officers (read: "knights") for trade and tradesmen was based on purely pragmatic reasons. Aside from ethical considerations, officers' elitism resulted, through practical political reality, in isolating them from the society they protected. This isolation, implemented in many ways, created a professional officer dependent on the service he served — one almost monastic in nature — interested only in his mission. "Duty, Honor, Country," it may be recalled, is the creed of the United States Military Academy at West Point. Today, however, with the military and the national industrial base so closely intertwined, this age-old custom is facing extinction.

A "democratic army" by definition is one *of* the people and should be drawn equally *from* the people, existing as a cadre in times of relative calm and expanded, when needed, through volunteerism, the calling up of reserves or the local militias (in the United States, the National Guard), or a just system of conscription. Each soldier has the vote in a democracy, and so do his family and friends. In the case of general mobilization or through a concomitant national conscription, concern for the well-being of members of the service becomes widespread. Unless there is a great sense of national purpose and unity, a government would be obliged to face growing questions about its rationale if it continued a costly war, even a "democratic" one.

Apart from its bringing a war "home" to a great number of people almost from the conflict's inception, a democratic army not under rigid control by its government and one without firm traditions of non-involvement in the political process poses problems at home in times of unrest. Any political eruptions in the forces, which would have been diverted or crushed in a small professional army isolated by tradition and with little political influence in the body politic, would ripple and then surge through an entire population.

*   *   *

The people who had settled Brooklyn were never a very war-like race. The Dutch wanted to work hard and enjoy the fruits of their labors; they did not wish to trouble their neighbors and prayed their neighbors would return the favor. The Dutch kept slaves, but, in their particular view of things, slaves were indeed human beings and allowed through their work to earn money and buy their freedom. And in the Dutch idea of citizenship anyone who paid his or her own way and didn't trouble others was entitled to full participation in the community.

The Dutch, as well as the other settlers of the western part of Long Island who had come from the British Isles and the Caribbean, as well as the freed slaves, had perhaps a better life before the Revolutionary War, under the relatively indolent rule of the British Crown. There was an official church, but one which did not interfere with the Dutch settlers' practice of their own faith or that of the dissenters in Gravesend or the Quakers on the North Shore. Business was, for the most part, unregulated. There had been a general climate of prosperity for those who would work for it.

According to commentaries at the time, those settlers on the mainland — which meant any part of the outland beyond the Hudson or Harlem Rivers, or perhaps the East River — were viewed as contentious people in matters of law and politics. Brooklyn was never known as a hotbed of revolution. Neither was it a Tory stronghold. With the passing of the Redcoats across the East River, perhaps the residents of the borough believed that they could look for the old untroubled, quiet, good life of the *status quo ante*..

Postscript

THE OLD STONE HOUSE at Gowanus, built in 1699 by Nicholas Vechte, which became the site of the Marylanders' action, was used as the first clubhouse of the baseball team to be known as the Brooklyn Dodgers, when the area surrounding it was called Washington Park. The house was destroyed in a military demonstration of Gatling guns and buried during street grading and park leveling operations in the 1890s, and was first rebuilt in the 1930s. Thereafter, it served over the years — despite successive vandalism and gross neglect — as a facility of the surrounding athletic fields of J.J. Byrne Park, named after a Brooklyn Borough president. At this writing it is being restored anew to serve as an educational center operated by the First Battle Revival Alliance, a group seeking to preserve the memory of that day in late August, 1776.

A number of monuments have been erected to commemorate the battle. Some — those in private hands — have fared well, such as the bas-relief plaque of a mounted George Washington on the Independence Savings Bank at Court Street and Atlantic Avenue (the site of the Cobble Hill fort) — and the earlier described Altar to Liberty on Battle Hill in Green-Wood Cemetery, where the Battle of Long Island Memorial Committee commemorates the event each year. And there is a plaque at the Flatlands Reform Church on Kings Highway east of Flatbush Avenue.

The Prison Ships Martyrs' Monument, in Fort Greene Park, the world's tallest freestanding Doric column, is tended and kept relatively graffiti-free by the New York City Department of Parks and Recreation.

It was designed by architect Stanford White, along with its monumental staircase, its visitors' center and its vault. The burial chamber contains the remains of the some 11,000 Americans who died in the British prison hulks anchored in Wallabout Bay during the seven years of occupation. The area surrounding this monument is the site of the strongest point of the inner defenses during the Brooklyn battle.

Another monument by Stanford White, a marble shaft topped with a sphere in memory of the Marylanders, has fared less well. Originally a gift of the Maryland Society of the Sons of the American Revolution, it was erected in 1895, later restored by the Maryland government and rededicated in 1991. It stands to the west of the lake in Prospect Park and on the slope of Lookout Hill.

There are plaques at Battle Pass, repeatedly vandalized and occasionally stolen for their value as scrap metal. The words they contain attest more to their sponsors' good intentions than to a thorough knowledge of the battle. The Michael Rawley, Jr., American Legion Post, No. 1636, at Third Avenue and Ninth Street on part of the land where Stirling made his stand and near the site of the mass grave of the Marylanders, bears a blue metal plaque, similar to those found at historic sites on roads throughout New York State. It reads: "New York / Maryland Heroes / Here Lie Buried 256 / Maryland Soldiers / Who Fell in the / Battle of Brooklyn / August 27th, 1776 / State Education / Department 1952."

The actual site of the grave, once on Adrian Van Brunt's farm, is on Third Avenue between Seventh and Eighth Streets. Once the court-yard of a Red Devil Paint factory, the site is now occupied by an automobile repair shop. Here, on the Sunday closest to August 27th, a small group of people from the Society of Old Brooklynites regularly holds a quiet memorial service. The building is not marked.

*   *   *

Today, long after the War of Independence, the events of the battle are remembered on the map of Brooklyn. Howe's route to the Jamaica Pass remains King's Highway; but Clinton Street and Avenue were named after a governor of New York State, not a child born in the colony of New York who later became the British Commander-in-Chief in America.

General Greene has an avenue and, as a remembrance of the star-shaped fort, the Fort Greene Park; Putnam also has an avenue.

The Marylanders' sacrifice was commemorated in the name of a community, Carroll Gardens, as well as Carroll Street, after statesman Charles Carroll of Carrolltown, Maryland, who sent the troops (and signed the Declaration of Independence). There is also the misspelled Sterling Place and Street.

General Washington came out better here than did Napoleon in Paris. The French capital has a Rue Bonaparte; but Brooklyn has its Washington Avenue and Street, and had, for a time, Washington Park.

29. The Old Stone House at Gowanus. Above, pictured in 1870, before its destruction. **30.** Below, the reconstructed house as it appears today, soon to be a visitors' center.

31. The Narrows, between Brooklyn and Staten Island, now spanned by the Verrazano Bridge.

32. The reconstructed Lefferts Homestead in Brooklyn. Lefferts' house was originally burned by forward units of Pennsylvanians during the battle.

33. The Port Road today. This was the main route for the Hessian columns who burst through Battle Pass and pursued the Americans to the Gowanus.

34. Formerly a swampy creek, the Gowanus Canal today bears little resemblance to a natural body of water.

35. Battle Pass in Prospect Park.

36. A walking path near Battle Pass, with terrain and foliage little changed since the time of the battle.

37. The Prison Ship Martyrs Monument, built, in Fort Greene Park, to
commemorate the thousands of Americans who died in British prison ships
during the Revolution. The unluckiest, perhaps, were those prisoners taken at
Brooklyn, the first major battle fought by the United States.

38. On the site of the Cobble Hill fort stands Independence Savings Bank.

39. Fulton Landing, at the foot of the Brooklyn Bridge, is the site of the evacuation of Washington's army to Manhattan.

40. The dedication, in 1920, of The Altar to Liberty, on Battle Hill in Green-Wood Cemetery.

41. The Monument to Maryland's Four Hundred, in Prospect Park. Designed by Stanford White and dedicated in 1895, the monument was restored by the State of Maryland in 1991.

Appendix A

American Order of Battle

Units in the New York Theater — Brooklyn, Manhattan, Westchester and Long Island.

Commander-in-Chief: George Washington

Aides-de-Camp: Col. William Grayson, Va.; Lieut. Col. Richard Cary, Jr., Mass.; Lieut. Col. Samuel B. Webb, Conn.; Lieut. Tench Tighman, Penn. Secretary: Lieut. Col. Robert Hanson Harrison, Va.

Adjutant General: Col. Joseph Reed, Penn. Quartermaster General: Col. Stephen Moylan, Penn. Commissary General: Col. Joseph Trumbull, Conn. Paymaster General: Col. William Palfrey, Mass. Muster-Master General: Col. Gunning Bedford, Penn. Director of the General Hospital: Dr. John Morgan, Penn. Chief Engineer: Col. Rufus Putnam, Mass.

Commander of Artillery: Col. Henry Knox, Mass.

Commanding in Brooklyn: Maj. Gen. Israel Putnam

PUTNAM'S DIVISION
Maj. Gen. Israel Putnam (Maj. Aaron Burr, a.d.c.)

Brig. Gen. James Clinton (David Henley, Major of Brigade)
    13th Cont. (Mass.) Col. Joseph Read
    3rd Cont. (Mass.) Col. Ebenezer Learned
    23rd Cont. (Mass.) Col. John Bailey
    26th Cont. (Mass.) Col. Loammi Baldwin

Brig. Gen. John Morin Scott (Nicholas Fish MoB)
   1st Independent Bn. (N.Y.) Col. John Lasher
   2nd N.Y. County Bn. (N.Y.) Col. William Malcolm (or Malcom)
   Militia (N.Y.) Col. Samuel Drake
   Militia (N.Y.) Col. Cornelius Humphrey

Brig. Gen. John Fellows (Mark Hopkins, MoB)
   Worcester County Militia (Mass.) Col. Jonathan Holman
   Plymouth and Bristol County Militia (Mass.) Col. Simon Cary
   Berkshire County Militia (Mass.) Col. Jonathan Smith
   14th Cont. (Mass.) "The Marblehead Regiment," Col. John Glover

HEATH'S DIVISION
Maj. Gen. William Heath (Maj. Thomas Henly, Maj. Israel Keith,
   a.d.c.s)

Brig. Gen. Thomas Mifflin (Jonathan Mifflin, MoB)
   3rd Penn. Bn. (Penn.) Col. John Shee
   5th Penn. Bn. (Penn.) Col. Robert Magaw
   16th Cont. (Mass.) Col. Paul Dudley Sargent
   27th Cont. (Mass.) Col. Israel Hutchinson
   Ward's Bn. (Conn.) Col. Andrew Ward

Brig. Gen. George Clinton (Albert Pawling, MoB)
   Militia (N.Y.) Col. Thomas Thomas
   Militia (N.Y.) Col. Isaac Nichol
   Militia (N.Y.) Col. James Swartwout
   Militia (N.Y.) Col. Levi Paulding (or Palding)
   Militia (N.Y.) Col. Morris Graham

SPENCER'S DIVISION
Maj. Gen. Joseph Spencer (Maj. William Peck, Maj. Charles Whiting,
   a.d.c.s)

Brig. Gen. Samuel Holden Parsons (Thomas Dyer, MoB)
   10th Cont. (Conn.) Col. John Tyler
   17th Cont. (Conn.) Col. Jedediah Huntington
   20th Cont. (Conn.) Col. John Durkee
   21st Cont. (Mass.) Col. Jonathan Ward
   22nd Cont. (Conn.) Col. Samuel Wyllys

Brig. Gen. James Wadsworth (John Palsgrave Wyllys, MoB)
    Levies (Conn.) Col. Gold Selleck Silliman
    Levies (Conn.) Col. Fisher Gay
    Levies (Conn.) Col. Comfort Sage
    Levies (Conn.) Col. Samuel Selden
    Levies (Conn.) Col. William Douglas
    Levies (Conn.) Col. John Chester
    Levies (Conn.) Col. Phillip Burr Bradley

SULLIVAN'S DIVISION

Maj. Gen. John Sullivan (Maj. Alexander Scammell, Maj. Lewis Morris, Jr.,
    a.d.c.s)

Brig. Gen. William Alexander, Lord Stirling (W.S. Livingston, MoB)
    Maryland Rgt., "The Dandy Fifth" (Md.) Col. William Smallwood
        (Maj. Mordecai Gist)
    Delaware Bn. (Del.) Col. John Haslet (Maj. Thomas McDonough)
    Penn. Rifle Rgt. (Penn.) Col. Samuel Miles
    Penn. Musketeers (Penn.) Col. Samuel John Atlee
    Penn. Militia (Penn.) Lieut. Col. Peter Kachlein
    Lancaster County Militia (Penn.) Maj. Hay

Brig. Gen. Alexander McDougall (Richard Platt, MoB)
    1st N.Y. Rgt. (N.Y.) late McDougall's
    3rd N.Y. Rgt. (N.Y.) Col. Rudolph Retzema
    19th Cont. (Conn.) Col. Charles Webb
    Artificers (e.g., armorers, ammunition handlers) (Mass.) Col.
        Jonathan Brewer

GREENE'S DIVISION

Maj. Gen. Nathanael Greene (Maj. William Blodgett, Maj. William S.
    Livingston, a.d.c.s)

Brig. Gen. John Nixon (Daniel Box, MoB)
    1st Cont. (Penn.) Col. Edward Hand
    9th Cont. (R.I.) Col. James Mitchell Varnum
    11th Cont. (R.I.) Col. Daniel Hitchcock
    4th Colonial Infantry (Mass. Bn.) (Mass.) late Nixon's
    7th Colonial Infantry (Mass. Bn.), the "Bunker Hill Regiment" (Mass.)
        Col. William Prescott
    12th Cont. (Mass.) Col. Moses Little

Brig. Gen. Nathaniel Heard (Peter Gordon, MoB)
    New Levies (N.J.) Col. David Forman
    Militia (N.J.) Col. Philip Johnston
    New Levies (N.J.) Col. Ephraim Martin
    New Levies (N.J.) Col. Silas Newcomb
    New Levies (N.J.) Col. Phillip Van Cortlandt

CONNECTICUT MILITIA

    Militia (Conn.) Col. Baldwin
    Militia (Conn.) Col. Chapman
    Militia (Conn.) Col. Cooke
    Militia (Conn.) Col. Hinman
    Militia (Conn.) Col. Pettibone
    Militia (Conn.) Col. Talcott
    Militia (Conn.) Col. Thompson
    Militia (Conn.) Lieut. Col. Lewis
    Militia (Conn.) Lieut. Col. Mead
    Militia (Conn.) Lieut. Col. Pitkin
    Militia (Conn.) Maj. Strong
    Militia (Conn.) Maj. Newberry

LONG ISLAND MILITIA
Brig. Gen. Nathaniel Woodhull (Jonathan Lawrence, MoB)

    Suffolk County Militia (N.Y.) Col. Josiah Smith
    King's and Queen's County Militia (N.Y.) Col. Jeronimus Remsen

British Order of Battle

(In British and Continental armies the post of colonel or chief was often honorary although the holder of the position may have taken an active part in the unit's operations. The regiment was usually commanded in the field by a lieutenant colonel. Listed here are those colonels who actually served in the New York theater.)

Commander-in-Chief: Sir William Howe

CLINTON'S DIVISION
Lieut. Gen. Sir Henry Clinton

Brig. Gen. Alexander Leslie (or Lesslie) (Lewis, Major of Brigade)
    3rd Bgt. Light Inf.
    1st Bat. Light Inf.
    2nd Bat. Light Inf.

CLEVELAND'S DIVISION
Brig. Gen. Samuel Cleveland (Farrington, MoB)
    1st Bgd. Art.
    2nd Bgd. Art.
    3rd Bgd. Art.

FIRST LINE
Maj. Gen. James Robertson, 1st Bgd. (Smith, MoB)
    4th Rgt. of Foot (The King's Own), Lieut. Col. Harry Blunt
    15th Rgt. of Foot

27th Rgt. of Foot (Eniskillings), Lieut. Col. John Maxwell
45th Rgt. of Foot, Col. James Cunninghame commanding

Maj. Gen. Robert Pigot, 2nd Bgd. (Disney, MoB)
    5th Rgt. of Foot, Colonel, Lieut. Gen. Percy, Lieut. Col. William
        Walcott commanding.
    28th Rgt. of Foot
    35th Rgt. of Foot
    49th Rgt. of Foot, Lieut. Col. Sir Henry Calder, Bt.

Maj. Gen. James Agnew, 6th Bgd. (Leslie, MoB)
    23rd Rgt. of Foot
    44th Rgt. of Foot
    57th Rgt. of Foot
    64th Rgt. of Foot

Brig. Gen. Francis Smith, 5th Bgd. (McKenzie, MoB)
    22nd Rgt. of Foot
    43rd Rgt. of Foot, Lieut. Col. George Clerk
    54th Rgt. of Foot, Lieut. Col. Alured Clark
    63rd Rgt. of Foot, Lieut. Col. James Paterson

Maj. Gen Edward Mathews (or Mathew)
    1st Bn. Guards
    2nd Bn. Guards

The cavalry on the flanks included the 17th Light Dragoons, Maj. Gen.
George Preston commanding.

SECOND LINE
Lieut. Gen. Hugh Earl Percy

Maj. Gen. James Grant, 4th Bgd. (Brown, MoB)
    17th Rgt. of Foot, Col. John Darby commanding
    40th Rgt. of Foot, Lieut. Col. James Grant
    46th Rgt. of Foot, Colonel, Gen. Sir William Howe, Col. the Hon.
        John Vaughn commanding, Lieut. Col. Enoch Markham
    55th Rgt. of Foot, Colonel, Maj. Gen. James Grant, Lieut. Col.
        William Meadows commanding

Maj. Gen. Valentine Jones, 3rd Bgd. (Baker, MoB)
    10th Rgt. of Foot, Lieut. Col. Francis Smith

37th Rgt. of Foot
38th Rgt. of Foot
52nd Rgt. of Foot, late Jones'

Brig. Gen. William Erskine (Erskine, MoB)
    1st Bn. 71st Fraser Highlanders, Lieut. Col. the Hon. John Maitland
    2nd Bn. 71st Fraser Highlanders, Col. Alexander, Earl of Balcarres
        commanding
    3rd Bn. 71st Fraser Highlanders

RESERVES
Lieut. Gen. Charles Earl Cornwallis
    1st Bn. Grenadiers
    2nd Bn. Grenadiers
    3rd Bn. Grenadiers
    4th Bn. Grenadiers
    33rd Rgt. of Foot, Colonel, Lieut. Gen. Charles Earl Cornwallis
    42nd, The Black Watch (Royal Highland Rgt.), Lieut. Col.
        Thomas Stirling (or Sterling)

Two units were listed as being under Howe's command, but not mentioned in the accounts of the period or included in other orders of battle: 7th Rgt. of Foot (Royal Fusiliers) and 16th Rgt. of Foot.

HESSIAN DIVISION
Lieut. Gen. Leopold Philip de Heister (or von Heister in some accounts), Baron Wilhelm von Knyphausen second in command. All German units in the action were from Hesse-Cassel.

Maj. Gen. von Mirbach
    Fusilier Rgt. von Knyphausen, Chief, Lieut. Gen. W. von
        Knyphausen, Col. H. von Borck commanding
    Grenadiere Rgt. von Rall, Col. J.G. Rall commanding
    Lieb Infantry Rgt., Col. F.W. von Lossberg commanding
    Fusilier Rgt. von Lossberg, Col. H.A. von Heeringen commanding

Maj. Gen. J.D. von Stirn
    Musketeer Rgt. von Donop, Chief. Lieut. Gen. H.A. von Donop,
        Col. D.U. von Gosen commanding
    Musketeer Rgt. von Mirbach, Col. J.A. von Loos commanding

Fusilier Rgt. Erbprinz (Hereditary Prince), Maj. Gen. J.D. von Stirn
    commanding

Col. Emil Count von Donop
    Block Grenadiers
    3rd Battalion Grenadiere von Minegerode, Lieut. Col. von
        Minegerode
    Grenadiere Rgt. von Lisingen, Lieut. Col. O.C.W. von Lisingen
    Jaeger Corps, Col. C.E.C. von Donop commanding

Col. F.W. von Lossberg
    Fusilier Rgt. von Ditfurth, Col. C. von Bose commanding
    Musketeer Rgt. von Trumbach, Col. C.E. von Bischhausen
        commanding

Baron von Riedesel
    Dragoons

Additionally listed as serving with the British in the New York theater during the battle, but not mentioned in any orders of battle, is the Musketeer
Rgt. Prinz Carl, Maj. Gen. M.C. Schmidt commanding. However, this unit
may be one of the number of regiments from Hesse-Cassel which arrived
shortly after the Battle of Brooklyn and took place in the actions in
Manhattan and Westchester.

Citations

INTRODUCTION
1. McPherson, *Battle Cry of Freedom,* p 809.

CHAPTER I
1. Heller and Stofft, *America's First Battles,* p. 14.
2. Kammen, *Colonial New York,* p. 369.
3. Ibid., p. 370.
4. *Dictionary of National Biography,* Vol. IX, p. 103.
5. Kammen, *Colonial New York,* p. 338.
6. Dupuy, *Governors Island,* p. 50.
7. Scheer and Rankin, *Rebels and Redcoats,* p. 146.
8. Luke and Venebles, *Long Island in the American Revolution,* pp. 8 and 9.
9. Ibid., pp. 10 and 11.
10. Ibid.
11. Bliven, *Under the Guns,* p. 45.
12. *Newsday,* "Long Island: The Way It Was," p. 13.
13. *Dictionary of National Biography,* Vol. IX, p. 103.
14. Onderdonk, *Revolutionary Incidents in Queens County,* p. 81.

CHAPTER II
1. Johnston, *The Campaign of 1776,* pp. 47 and 48.
2. *Newsday,* "Long Island: The Way It Was," p. 8.
3. Johnston, *The Campaign of 1776,* p. 46.
4. Kobrin, *The Black Minority in Early New York,* p. 11.
5. Miller, *Brooklyn, U.S.A.,* p. 78.
6. Ibid., p. 71.

CHAPTER III
1. Lancaster, *American Heritage History of the American Revolution*, p. 171.
2. Turner, *A History of Military Affairs*, p. 94.
3. Booth, *The Women of '76*, p. 125.
4. Ketchum, *American Heritage Book of the Revolution*, p. 156.

CHAPTER IV
1. Heller and Stofft, *America's First Battles*, p. 12.
2. Ibid.
3. Turner, *A History of Military Affairs*, p. 155.
4. Flick, *The American Revolution in New York*, p. 140.
5. Lancaster, *American Heritage History of the American Revolution*, p. 172.
6. Flint, *Long Island Before the Revolution*, p. 393.
7. Lancaster, *American Heritage History of the American Revolution*, p. 168.
8. Ibid., p. 147.
9. Fraser, *The Stone House at Gowanus*, p. 106.
10. Glas, "The Long, Long Rifle," p. 43.
11. Hofstadter, "America as a Gun Culture," p. 10.
12. Stiles, *History of the City of Brooklyn*, Vol. I, p. 281.
13. Scheer and Rankin, *Rebels and Redcoats*, p. 159.
14. Wertenbaker, *Father Knickerbocker Rebels*, p. 92.
15. Stiles, *History of the City of Brooklyn*, Vol. I, p. 295.

CHAPTER V
1. Scheer and Rankin, *Rebels and Redocats*, pp. 155 and 156.
2. Ibid., p. 156.
3. Ibid.
4. Ibid., pp. 156 and 157.
5. Ibid., pp. 157 and 158.
6. Pearson, *Those Damned Rebels*, pp. 157 and 158.
7. Scheer and Rankin, *Rebels and Redcoats*, p. 158.
8. Ibid.
9. *Newsday*, "Long Island: The Way It Was," p. 8.
10. Demeritt, "The Battle of Long Island," n.p.
11. Manhoffer, "Eyewitness 1776," p. 3.
12. Bliven, *Under the Guns*, p. 330.
13. Great Britain Historical Manuscripts Commission, *Report on . . . Reginald Rawdon Hastings, III*, pp. 179 and 180.
14. Ibid.
15. Freeman, *George Washington*, p. 85.
16. Henshaw, *Orderly Books, October 1, 1775 . . . October 3, 1776*, p. 219.
17. Ibid., p. 131.

CHAPTER VI
1. Adams, *The Battle of Long Island,* pp. 650 and 651.
2. Bliven, *Under the Guns,* p. 319.
3. Stiles, *History of the City of Brooklyn,* Vol. I, p. 248.
4. Adams, *The Battle of Long Island,* p. 653.
5. Flint, *Long Island Before the Revolution,* p. 372.
6. Ibid.
7. Hurley with Collin, "The Battle of Long Island," p. 2.
8. Boatner, *Encyclopedia of the American Revolution,* p. 649.
9. Heller and Stofft, *America's First Battles,* p. 24.

CHAPTER VII
1. Pearson, *Those Damned Rebels,* p. 163.
2. Scheer and Rankin, *Rebels and Redcoats,* p. 161.
3. Flint, *Long Island Before the Revolution,* p. 407.
4. Lancaster, *American Heritage History of the American Revolution,* p. 180.
5. Flint, *Long Island Before the Revolution,* p. 48.
6. Onderdonk, *Revolutionary Incidents of Suffolk and Kings Counties,* p. 133.
7. Ibid., pp. 133 and 134.
8. Lowell, *The Hessians and Other German Auxiliaries of Great Britain,* p. 61.
9. Onderdonk, *Revolutionary Incidents of Suffolk and Kings Counties,* p. 134.
10. Adams, *The Battle of Long Island,* p. 667.
11. Flint, *Long Island Before the Revolution,* p. 392.
12. Lowell, *The Hessians and Other German Auxiliaries of Great Britain,* p. 61.
13. Stiles, *History of the City of Brooklyn,* Vol. I, pp. 254 and 255.
14. Flint, *Long Island Before the Revolution,* pp. 391 and 392.
15. Fraser, *The Stone House at Gowanus,* p. 62.
16. Stiles, *History of the City of Brooklyn,* Vol. I, p. 259.

CHAPTER VIII
1. Fraser, *The Stone House at Gowanus,* p. 63.
2. Stiles, *History of the City of Brooklyn,* Vol. I, p. 268.
3. Adams, *The Battle of Long Island,* p. 667.
4. Stiles, *History of the City of Brooklyn,* Vol. I, p. 269.
5. Onderdonk, *Revolutionary Incidents of Suffolk and Kings Counties,* p. 147.
6. Fraser, *The Stone House at Gowanus,* p. 64.
7. Bergen, "The Rising Sun Tavern and the Rockaway Pass," p. 475.
8. Ibid., p. 476.
9. Ibid., pp. 473 and 474.
10. Stiles, *History of the City of Brooklyn,* Vol. I, p. 266.
11. Bergen, "The Rising Sun Tavern and the Rockaway Pass," p. 474.
12. Adams, *The Battle of Long Island,* p. 667.

13. Heller and Stofft, *America's First Battles*, p. 25.
14. Stiles, *History of the City of Brooklyn*, Vol. I, p. 267.

CHAPTER IX

1. Flint, *Long Island Before the Revolution*, p. 396.
2. Scheer and Rankin, *Rebels and Redcoats*, p. 166.
3. Martin, *A Narrative of Some of the Adventures . . . of a Revolutionary Soldier*, p. 19.
4. Ibid., pp. 19, 20 and 21.
5. Manhoffer, "Eyewitness 1776," p. 4.
6. Ketchum, *American Heritage Book of the Revolution*, p. 150.
7. Onderdonk, *Revolutionary Incidents of Suffolk and Kings Counties*, p. 147.
8. Great Britain Historical Manuscripts Commission, *Report on . . . Reginald Rawdon Hastings, III*, p. 181.
9. Dupuy, *Governors Island*, p. 59.
10. Stiles, *History of the City of Brooklyn*, Vol. I, p. 275.
11. Dupuy, *Governors Island*, p. 52.
12. Heller and Stofft, *America's First Battles*, p. 26.
13. Ibid.
14. Flint, *Long Island Before the Revolution*, pp. 408 and 409.
15. Stiles, *History of the City of Brooklyn*, pp. 274 and 275.
16. Scheer and Rankin, *Rebels and Redcoats*, p. 167.
17. Onderdonk, *Revolutionary Incidents of Suffolk and Kings Counties*, p. 138.
18. Stiles, *History of the City of Brooklyn*, Vol. I, p. 274.
19. Ibid.
20. Ibid., p. 281.

CHAPTER X

1. Onderdonk, *Revolutionary Incidents of Suffolk and Kings Counties*, p. 147.
2. Heller and Stofft, *America's First Battles*, p. 26.
3. Onderdonk, *Revolutionary Incidents of Suffolk and Kings Counties*, pp. 151 and 152.
4. Ibid., p. 152.
5. Ibid.
6. Flint, *Long Island Before the Revolution*, p. 396.
7. Scheer and Rankin, *Rebels and Redcoats*, p. 167.
8. Stiles, *History of the City of Brooklyn*, Vol. I, p. 270.
9. Onderdonk, *Revolutionary Incidents of Suffolk and Kings Counties*, pp. 147 and 148.
10. Ibid., pp. 145 and 146.
11. Ibid., pp. 154 and 155.
12. Wertenbaker, *Father Knickerbocker Rebels*, p. 93.

13. Onderdonk, *Revolutionary Incidents of Suffolk and Kings Counties*, p. 155.
14. Ibid., p. 148.

CHAPTER XI
1. Dupuy, *Governors Island*, p. 52.
2. Lowell, *The Hessians and Other German Auxiliaries of Great Britain*, p. 65.
3. Flint, *Long Island Before the Revolution*, p. 409.
4. Booth, *The Women of '76*, p. 93.
5. Scheer and Rankin, *Rebels and Redcoats*, p. 167.
6. Stiles, *History of the City of Brooklyn*, Vol. I, p. 282.
7. Stevenson and Wilson, *The Battle of Long Island*, p. 18.
8. Smith, *Governors Island: Its Military History*, p. 57.
9. Stiles, *History of the City of Brooklyn*, Vol. I, p. 277.
10. Onderdonk, *Revolutionary Incidents of Suffolk and Kings Counties*, p. 165.
11. Stiles, *History of the City of Brooklyn*, Vol. I, p. 253.
12. *Dictionary of National Biography*, Vol. IX, p. 103.
13. Wright, *The Continental Army*, p. 20.
14. Flint, *Long Island Before the Revolution*, p. 409.
15. Onderdonk, *Revolutionary Incidents of Suffolk and Kings Counties*, p. 138.
16. Dupuy, *Governors Island*, p. 52.
17. Onderdonk, *Revolutionary Incidents of Suffolk and Kings Counties*, p. 158.
18. Ibid., p. 161.
19. Ibid., pp. 155 and 156.
20. Ibid., pp. 161.
21. Ibid., p. 151.

CHAPTER XII
1. Barck, *New York City During the War for Independence*, p. 232.
2. Onderdonk, *Revolutionary Incidents of Suffolk and Kings Counties*, pp. 161 and 162.
3. Ibid., p. 156.
4. Ibid., p. 151.
5. Adams, *The Battle of Long Island*, p. 663.
6. Stiles, *History of the City of Brooklyn*, Vol. I, p. 287.
7. Onderdonk, *Revolutionary Incidents of Suffolk and Kings Counties*, p. 147.
8. Tallmadge, *Memoirs*, pp. 11 and 12.
9. Stiles, *History of the City of Brooklyn*, Vol. I, p. 288.
10. Onderdonk, *Revolutionary Incidents of Suffolk and Kings Counties*, p. 158.
11. Ibid., p. 168.
12. Ibid., p. 163.
13. Flint, *Long Island Before the Revolution*, pp. 409 and 410.
14. Tallmadge, *Memoirs*, pp. 11 and 12.
15. Ketchum, *American Heritage Book of the Revolution*, p. 182.

CHAPTER XIII

1. Scheer and Rankin, *Rebels and Redcoats*, p. 172.
2. Ibid., p. 173.
3. Heller and Stofft, *America's First Battles*, p. 26.
4. Ibid., pp. 25 and 26.
5. Boatner, *Encyclopedia of the American Revolution*, p. 665.
6. Adams, *The Battle of Long Island*, p. 651.
7. Heller and Stofft, *America's First Battles*, p. 15.
8. Manhoffer, "Eyewitness 1776," p. 4.
9. Boatner, *Encyclopedia of the American Revolution*, pp. 799 and 800.
10. Ibid., p. 583.
11. Smith, *A New Age Now Begins*, p. 763.
12. Boatner, *Encyclopedia of the American Revolution*, p. 584.
13. Ibid., p. 802.
14. Smith, *A New Age Now Begins*, p. 771.
15. Ibid.
16. Boatner, *Encyclopedia of the American Revolution*, p. 491.

CHAPTER XIV

1. Kammen, *Colonial New York*, p. 276.
2. Turner, *History of Military Affairs in Western Society*, p. 48.

Bibliography

Adams, Charles Francis, Jr. *The Battle of Long Island* (reprinted from *American Historical Review*, Vol. I, July 1896).

Anonymous. *Louisbourg in 1745 (Lettres d'un Habitant de Louisbourg)*, George M. Wrong, ed. University of Toronto Studies—History; Second Series, Vol. I. Toronto, 1897.

Aptheker, Herbert. *The American Revolution 1763-1783*. New York: International Publishers, 1960.

Asimov, Isaac. *The Birth of the United States 1763-1817*. Boston: Houghton Mifflin, 1974.

Barck, Oscar Theodore. *New York City During the War for Independence*. Port Washington, NY: Ira J. Friedman, 1966.

Beach, Edward L. *The United States Navy, 200 Years*. New York: Henry Holt, 1986.

Bliven, Bruce, Jr. *Battle for Manhattan*. New York: Harper & Row, 1956.

Bliven, Bruce, Jr. *Under the Guns: New York, 1775-1776*. New York: Harper & Row, 1972.

Boatner, Mark M. III. *The Encyclopedia of the American Revolution*. New York: David McKay Co., 1966.

Booth, Sally Smith. *The Women of '76*. New York: Hastings House, 1984.

Buel, Joy Day and Richard, Jr. *The Way of Duty: A Woman and Her Family in Revolutionary America*. New York: W.W. Norton, 1984.

Chambers's Encyclopaedia. Edinburgh: William & Robert Chambers Ltd, 1908.

Clausewitz, Karl von. *On War* (Rutledge & Kay Paul, London, 1908 translation). London: Penguin, 1968.

Dictionary of American Biography. New York: Scribners, 1964.

Dictionary of National Biography. London: Oxford University Press, 1938.

Downey, Fairfax. *Louisbourg: Key to a Continent.* Englewood Cliffs, NJ: Prentice-Hall, 1965.

Dupuy, Major R. Ernest, ed. *Governors Island: Its History and Development, 1637–1937.* New York: Governors Island Club, 1937.

Ellis, John. *The Social History of the Machine Gun.* New York: Pantheon Books, 1987.

Evans, Elizabeth. *Weathering the Storm: Women of the American Revolution.* New York: Scribners, 1975.

Flick, Alexander C., ed. *The American Revolution in New York: Its Political, Social and Economic Significance.* Port Washington, NY: Ira J.Friedman, 1967.

Flint, Martha Bockée. *Long Island Before the Revolution: A Colonial Story.* Port Washington, NY: Ira J. Friedman, 1967.

Fraser, Georgia. *The Stone House at Gowanus.* New York: Witter and Kintner, 1909.

Freeman, Douglas S. *George Washington: A Biography.* New York: Scribners, 1948–57.

Great Britain Historical Manuscript Commission. *Report on the Manuscripts of the Late Reginald Rawdon Hastings, III.* London: His Majesty's Stationery Office, 1928–47.

Gross, Robert A. *The Minutemen and Their World.* American Century Series. New York: Hill and Wang, 1976.

Heller, Charles E., and Stofft, William A., eds. *America's First Battles, 1776–1965.* Kansas City: University Press of Kansas, 1986.

Henshaw, William. *The Orderly Books, October 1, 1775 Through October 3, 1776.* Worcester, MA, 1948.

Irving, Washington. *The Collected Works of Washington Irving.* New York: Greystone Press, n.d.

Johnston, Henry P. *The Campaign of 1776 Around New York and Brooklyn.* Brooklyn: Long Island Historical Society, 1878.

Jomini, Antoine Henri. *The Art of War* (J.B. Lippincott, Philadelphia, 1862 translation). Westport, CT: Greenwood Press, n.d.

Kammen, Michael. *A Rope of Sand: The Colonial Agents, British Politics and the American Revolution.* New York: Vintage, 1974.

Kammen, Michael. *Colonial New York: A History.* New York: Scribners, 1975.

Katcher, Philip R.N. *Encyclopedia of British, Provincial and German Auxiliary Units 1775–1783.* Harrisburg, PA: Stackpole Books, 1973.

Ketchum, Richard M., ed. *The American Heritage Book of the Revolution.* New York: American Heritage, 1958.

Kobrin, David. *The Black Minority in Early New York.* Albany: University of the State of New York, 1971.

Lancaster, Bruce. *From Lexington to Liberty: The Story of the American Revolution.* Garden City, NY: Doubleday, 1955.

Lancaster, Bruce. *The American Heritage History of the American Revolution.* New York: American Heritage, 1975.

Lancaster, Bruce. *The American Revolution.* New York: American Heritage, 1985.

Long Island Historical Society. *Memoirs II.* Brooklyn, 1869.

Lowell, Edward J. *The Hessians and Other German Auxiliaries of Great Britain in the Revolutionary War.* New York: Harper, 1884.

Luke, Myron H., and Venebles, Robert W. *Long Island in the American Revolution.* Albany: New York State American Revolution Bicentennial Commission, 1976.

Martin, Joseph P. *A Narrative of Some of the Adventures, Dangers and Sufferings of a Revolutionary Soldier.* Hallowell, ME, 1830. (Republished as *Private Yankee Doodle* by Joseph Plum Martin, New York: Little Brown, 1962.)

McCague, James. *The Second Rebellion: The New York City Draft Riots of 1863.* New York: Dial Press, 1968.

McPherson, James M. *Battle Cry of Freedom: The Civil War Era.* New York: Oxford University Press, 1988.

Miller, Rita Seidon, ed. *Brooklyn, U.S.A.* Brooklyn College Press, 1979.

Mollo, John. *Uniforms of the American Revolution.* New York: Macmillan, 1975.

Morgan, Edmund S., ed. *The American Revolution: Two Centuries of Interpretation.* Englewood Cliffs, NJ: Prentice-Hall, 1965.

New-York Historical Society. *Narratives of the Revolution in New York.* New York, 1975.

Onderdonk, Henry. *Revolutionary Incidents of Suffolk and Kings Counties.* New York, 1844. (Republished by Ira J. Friedman Division, Kennikat Press, Port Washington, NY, 1970.)

Onderdonk, Henry. *Revolutionary Incidents in Queens County.* New York, 1846. (Republished by Ira J. Friedman Division, Kennikat Press, Port Washington, NY, 1970.)

Pearson, Michael. *Those Damned Rebels: The American Revolution Through British Eyes.* New York: G.P. Putnam's Sons, 1974.

Ros, Martin. *Night of Fire: The Black Napoleon and the Battle for Haiti.* New York: Sarpedon, 1994.

Scheer, George F., and Rankin, Hugh F. *Rebels and Redcoats.* Cleveland and New York: World Publishing, 1957.

Schmizzi, Ernest and Gregory. *The Staten Island Peace Conference, September 11, 1776.* Albany: New York State Bicentennial Commission, 1976.

Serle, Ambrose. *The American Journal: Secretary to Lord Howe, 1776–1778,* Edward H. Tatum, Jr., ed. San Marino, CA, 1940.

Smith, Edmund Banks. *Governors Island: Its Military History Under Three Flags, 1637–1922.* New York: Valentine's Manual, 1923.

Smith, Page. *A New Age Now Begins: A People's History of the American Revolution.* New York: McGraw Hill, 1976.

Stevenson, Charles C., and Wilson, Irene H. *The Battle of Long Island, The Battle of Brooklyn.* The Brooklyn Bicentennial Committee, 1975.

Stiles, Henry R. *History of the City of Brooklyn,* Vol. I. Brooklyn, 1867.

Tallmadge, Benjamin. *Memoirs,* Henry P. Johnson, ed. New York: Sons of the Revolution in the State of New York Publications, 1904.

Trevelyan, Sir George Otto. *The American Revolution,* Vol. II. New York: Longmans, Green, 1905.

Tuchman, Barbara W. *The First Salute.* New York: Alfred A. Knopf, 1988.

Turner, Gordon B., ed. *A History of Military Affairs in Western Society Since the Eighteenth Century.* New York: Harcourt, Brace, 1952.

Wertenbaker, Thomas Jefferson. *Father Knickerbocker Rebels: New York City During the Revolution.* New York: Scribners, 1948.

Wright, Robert K., Jr. *The Continental Army.* Washington, DC: Center of Military History, United States Army, 1986.

ARTICLES AND PAMPHLETS

Bergen, T. G. "The Rising Sun Tavern and the Rockaway Pass," in *Manual of the Common Council of Brooklyn,* 1868.

"Dedication of Monument and Altar to Liberty on Battle Hill Greenwood (*sic*) Cemetery, August 27th, 1920." Brooklyn: Kings County Historical Society, 1920.

Demeritt, Dwight B., Jr. "The Battle of Long Island." Brooklyn: The Long Island Historical Society, 1967.

Glas, Herb. "The Long, Long Rifle," in *The American Gun* (Spring 1961).

Hofstadter, Richard. "America as a Gun Culture," in *American Heritage: The Magazine of History* (October 1970).

Hurley, James P., with Collin, Jane H. "The Battle of Long Island, Program of the Bicentennial Exhibit & Bird's Eye View of the City." Brooklyn: Williamsburgh Savings Bank, 1976.

"Long Island: The Way it Was." Excerpts from special section of *Newsday*, Melville, NY, 1976.

Manhoffer, Barbara. "Eyewitness 1776." Hicksville, NY: Long Island Lighting Company, 1982.

Index

ILLUSTRATION ACKNOWLEDGMENTS

The publishers are indebted to the following institutions and individuals for their courtesy in permitting use of the illustrations in this work:

Spencer Collection, The New York Public Library, Astor, Lenox and Tilden Foundations: (3) "View of the Narrows between Long Island & Staten Island, with our Fleet at Anchor & Lord Howe coming in (12th July 1776)"; (4) "18th June 1776"; (5) "View of the Rebel Work round Walton's House with Hele Gate" all by Archibald Robertson (plates 37, 33 and 43, respectively, from Robertson Diaries and Sketches).

Emmet Collection, Miriam and Ira D. Wallach Division of Art, Prints and Photographs, The New York Public Library, Astor, Lenox and Tilden Foundations: (7) "Honorable Sir William Howe," anonymous British artist.

I.N. Phelps Stokes Collection, Miriam and Ira D. Wallach Division of Art, Prints and Photographs, The New York Public Library, Astor, Lenox and Tilden Foundations: (11) "The Phoenix and the Rose Engaged by the Enemy's Fire Ships and Galleys on the 16 August, 1776," Dominic Serves from a sketch by Sir James Wallace.

Eno Collection, Miriam and Ira D. Wallach Division of Art, Prints and Photographs, The New York Public Library, Astor, Lenox and Tilden Foundations: (27) "Entrée Triumphale de Troupes royales à Nouvelle Yorck," by Francois Xavier Habermann.

The Brooklyn Historical Society: (25) "The Battle of Long Island," by Alonzo Chappel; (6) "The Redoubt at Valley Grove"; (12) "Denyse's Ferry"; Photos 29 and 40, from Old Brooklyn in Early Photographs 1865–1929, by William Lee Younger; Dover Publications, 1978.

The Pennsylvania Academy of the Fine Arts, Philadelphia: (8) "George Washington at Princeton," by Charles Willson Peale. Gift of Maria McKean Allen and Phebe Warren Downes through the bequest of their mother, Elizabeth Wharton McKean.

The Anne S. K. Brown Military Collection, Brown University Library: (14) "Lord Stirling's Last Struggle Around the Old Cortelyou House," by Alonzo Chappel; (24) "Lord Stirling at the Battle of Long Island," by Alonzo Chappel.

The Military Department, State of Maryland: (15) "The Departure of Smallwood's Battalion for New York, July 1776."

The Connecticut State Library, Hartford: (17) "Israel Putnam," sketch by John Trumbull, 1790.

The Maryland Historical Trust: (41) Photograph by Nancy Kurtz.

The National Maritime Museum, London: (13) "The Royal Navy in New York Harbour, 1776"; (19) "Occupation of Newport," by Robert Cleveley.

The Maryland State Archives, Commission on Artistic Property: (16) "Mordecai Gist," MSA SC 1545-1066; Peter E. Egeli copy after Charles Willson Peale portrait.
Dover Publications: (1) Engraving of a painting by M.A. Wageman; (2) Illustration by Howard Pyle in *Harper's Weekly*, Dec. 25, 1880; (10, 28) Howard Pyle for *Harper's Weekly*, 1858. Illustrations 9, 20, 21, 22 and 26.
John J. Gallagher: Photographs 30–36, 38 and 39.

The publishers would also like to express their deepest appreciation to Wilda Harrison Gallagher for the ten original maps created for this book, which appear on pages 28, 34, 62, 76, 90, 104, 112, 120, 128 and 152. Special thanks are also due Donn Teal, for research and fact-checking, Russell Bianca and Julius Weil, for graphic arts assistance, and to Sherrel Farnsworth and Emily Smith, for illustration research.